'A remarkable achie[ve]ment... guides the reader thr[ough] ... Reformation to the pre[sent] ... perception, precision and knowledge. This accessible story of the life of the Kirk in Scotland answers fundamental questions about what the Church of Scotland has been and is today and how it has shaped Scottish life and identity. Anyone and everyone interested in Scotland would benefit from reading this book.'

Jane Dawson, John Laing Professor of
Reformation History, University of Edinburgh

'The history of Scotland over the past millennium is inextricably linked with that of the Kirk and in this wonderfully accessible book, Finlay Macdonald provides a history of the Kirk until the present. But this is much, much more than just a history book. Macdonald explains the politico-religious and legal debates imbuing Scottish society for centuries and throughout brings to life the theological context – changing over time but continually important. At times one concludes there is not one Scotland but many and, while true of many countries, Finlay Macdonald finishes with an intriguing vision of a one-Scotland future. A real page turner and one I will return to time and again.'

Sir Ian Diamond, Principal and Vice-Chancellor,
University of Aberdeen

'This book should be essential reading for those who want to know something about the DNA of the Church of Scotland. In reading it we may see some repeating patterns of behaviour and in reading it carefully we may avoid repeating some of our worst excesses. Finlay Macdonald has used both his knowledge and his affection for the Church to give us an accessible history of four centuries of our life and, for many years to come, this will be a textbook for the ordinary member who wants to better understand what has made us what we are.'

Very Revd Dr John Chalmers, Principal Clerk of the General Assembly of the Church of Scotland

'You couldn't ask for a better guide to lead you down the highways – and by-ways – of the history of the Church of Scotland than Finlay Macdonald. Grounded in solid historical scholarship and his first-hand knowledge of the workings of the Kirk, this is an accessible and concise history highlighting the controversies and debates, century by century, which formed the Church as it is today. Finlay Macdonald writes with insight and a lightness of touch. A fine book for the interested general reader and a good refresher for those who have forgotten about the "Auld Lichts" and "New Lichts".'

Revd Calum MacLeod, Minister of St Giles' Cathedral, Edinburgh

'A fascinating account of the history of the Church of Scotland from the Reformation to the present. The reader is led through highs and lows, periods of peace and times of conflict illustrating how the Church has arrived at where it is today. Thoughtful connections between past and present make for an enjoyable and informative read. I highly commend this book to Church people and beyond.'

Very Revd Bill Hewitt, Joint Clerk of the Presbytery of Glasgow

FROM REFORM TO RENEWAL
Scotland's Kirk Century by Century

Finlay Macdonald

SAINT ANDREW PRESS

First published in 2017 by
SAINT ANDREW PRESS
121 George Street
Edinburgh EH2 4YN

Copyright © Finlay Macdonald 2017

ISBN 978 0 86153 976 5

The opinions expressed in this book are those of the author and do not necessarily
reflect those of the publisher.

Quotation from 'Look forward in faith' by Andrew J. Scobie, 2005, *Church
Hymnary 4*, Norwich: Canterbury Press. Used by permission.

Scripture quotations are from the New Revised Standard Version of the Bible,
Anglicized Edition, copyright © 1989, 1995 by the Division of Christian
Education of the National Council of the Churches of Christ in the USA. Used by
permission. All rights reserved.

British Library Cataloguing in Publication Data
A catalogue record for this book is available from the British Library.

It is the publisher's policy to only use papers that are natural and
recyclable and that have been manufactured from timber grown in renewable,
properly managed forests. All of the manufacturing
processes of the papers are expected to conform to the
environmental regulations of the country of origin.

Typeset by Mary Matthews
Printed and bound in the United Kingdom by CPI Group (UK) Ltd

CONTENTS

ACKNOWLEDGEMENTS

Some acknowledgements are appropriate. My particular thanks go to the distinguished Scottish historian Rosalind K. Marshall for her generous encouragement as this book took shape; also to Laura Dunlop, David Fergusson, Sheilagh Kesting and David Robertson for advice on issues relating to their particular fields of expertise, and to John Chalmers, Principal Clerk of the General Assembly and his staff in facilitating access to Assembly records. I am grateful to Ann Crawford of Saint Andrew Press at the time this book was forming in my mind, who encouraged me to develop the idea; also to Peter Backhouse for his generous assistance with photographs, and to Iain Whyte, Secretary of the Church of Scotland Guild, and Jane Bristow of the Church's Communications Department in this same connection. Finally, I place on record my thanks to Christine Smith and her team at Hymns Ancient & Modern for commissioning the book and for all their subsequent advice and assistance through the publication process.

PREFACE

The idea for this book came from various conversations which suggested that an accessible overview of the Kirk's story would be helpful for elders, church members and the general reader – perhaps even for ministers interested in a crash refresher course.

There are many detailed studies of momentous events and famous individuals, but what I offer here is a more general survey, highlighting and illustrating the main themes of each century since the Reformation. The style aims to be accessible; the tone affectionate but not uncritical. I also make connections back and forth as the story unfolds. Inevitably, not all will agree with my choices as to what to include and what to omit, but I have endeavoured to provide enough detail to give a fair picture of the Kirk's journey from the Reformation to the present. For those wishing to explore further there is a short bibliography with suggestions for further reading.

Finlay Macdonald
All Saints' Day, 2016

SETTING THE SCENE

In August 1560 the Scottish Parliament rejected the authority of the Pope and outlawed the celebration of the Mass. This was far from a sudden decision; rather it was a defining moment in a process that had been gathering pace over many years and that would continue to evolve. It was, though, a hugely significant step and effectively determined the date of the Scottish Reformation.

What lay behind the growing pressure for reform? Here are some of the questions people were asking:

- When the priest celebrated Mass, did the bread and wine actually become the body and blood of Christ?
- Was there a place called Purgatory, a kind of halfway state between Heaven and Hell where sins were purged?
- Why could the Bible not be available in the everyday language of the people?
- Why were church services in Latin?
- Why was there so much wealth in the upper echelons of the Church when so many ordinary people were poor?
- Why did so many supposedly celibate priests father children? Why couldn't they just marry?
- Why were sons of kings (including illegitimate sons) given lucrative church appointments, sometimes while they were still children?

Questions such as these lay behind the movement for church reform, not only in Scotland, but across Europe.

The term 'Kirk' has come to designate the reformed Church of Scotland which today is Presbyterian in government. The change from Roman Catholic to Presbyterian did not happen overnight. The Reformers didn't wake up one day and decide to start a new Church. Rather, over many years and decades they sought to make changes from within to the institution in which they had been nurtured from birth. It follows that, despite the sixteenth-century parting of ways, a vital element of the Kirk's self-understanding today is that it shares a common pre-Reformation history with the Roman Catholic Church. Today's Scottish Catholics and Protestants may differ on matters of doctrine but they share a common heritage through Columba, Mungo and others who first brought the Gospel to Scotland.

Sauchieburn to Flodden

One of the darkest days in Scottish history was 9 September 1513. On that day the Battle of Flodden was fought, resulting in the death of King James IV, along with many leading figures in the nation's life. Two particular battles stand out in Scottish history – Bannockburn in 1314 and Flodden in 1513. The former is celebrated in songs such as 'Scots Wha Hae'; the latter mourned in 'The Flowers of the Forest'.

Less well-known is the Battle of Sauchieburn, but it provides a good starting point for this narrative. James III, who reigned from 1460 to 1488, was an ineffective and unpopular king and a ready focus for rebellions. He and his queen, Margaret of Denmark, had three sons – the future James IV, James Stewart Duke of Ross (his father's favourite) and John Stewart. The king's ability to alienate extended even to his own family, and in 1488 matters came to a head at Sauchieburn, a few miles south of Stirling. King and heir fought on opposite sides of the battle and the king was killed as he fled the field. So at the age of fifteen, James IV came to the throne. Ever after, as a classic act of penance, he wore an iron belt round his waist, adding an additional weight each year.

Within two weeks of the battle James was crowned at Scone. The ceremony created new tensions, though this time of an ecclesiastical nature. Bishop Blackadder of Glasgow, who had supported the rebellion, was invited to place the crown on the king's head. This deeply offended Archbishop Schevez of St Andrews, who had been a loyal supporter of James III. Furthermore, only recently the Pope had recognised the primacy of the archdiocese of St Andrews. This meant that Schevez outranked Blackadder who was, after all, only a bishop. Surely as senior prelate he, Schevez, should have placed the crown on the king's head!

As it happened, the new king was a canon of the See of Glasgow, a typical example of the mingling of royal and ecclesiastical appointments. This explains the choice of Blackadder, who was busy campaigning to have Glasgow raised to an archbishopric. James supported this move and quickly had Parliament pass an Act declaring its support, and four years later, Pope Innocent VIII duly obliged, establishing Glasgow as an Archiepiscopal and Metropolitan See. However, the Pope stopped short of granting an additional request from James that the new archbishop be created a cardinal. He did, however, exempt Glasgow and its provinces from the jurisdiction of St Andrews. In the gesture one senses a papal concern that the prelates re-focus their energies on their primary task of promoting the Gospel. In truth, though, high ecclesiastical office brought an enhanced political role, and this was the real prize being fought over.

Meanwhile, James had his own game to play. If high-ranking ecclesiastics wished to exercise political power it was equally the case that high-ranking non-ecclesiastics were anxious to have some control over the Church; and there was none higher than the king. Having gained the throne through a rebellion against his father, James was anxious to protect his own back against future threats, not least from his younger brother, the Duke of Ross. When Archbishop Schevez died in 1497, James saw his opportunity and nominated the duke to be the next archbishop. Then, with the agreement of the Pope, he added lucrative commendatorships of Holyrood, Dunfermline and Arbroath to the duke's 'responsibilities'. These were effectively appointments to vacant monastic benefices giving title to the emoluments attached to them, thereby enhancing the royal revenues. An estimate of the comparative wealth of Church and Crown at the time suggests that ecclesiastical revenues were ten times greater than resources available to the Crown. From James' point of view he was simply restoring the balance, buying off a potential rival and securing his throne in some style. Then, in the spirit of 'the best laid schemes', the Duke of Ross died in 1504 at the age of twenty-eight. This circumstance did not entirely relieve James of anxiety over possible rivals, so he devised a new plan. This was to have his illegitimate son, Alexander Stewart, who was still in his teens, appointed Archbishop of St Andrews. Two years previously Pope Julius II had approved the youth's appointment as Administrator of the archdiocese. In addition to these lucrative roles, young Alexander was to receive the revenues of Dunfermline Abbey and Coldingham Priory and to take on the office of Chancellor of the Kingdom. As James was acting as his son's guardian, again it was the Crown that ultimately benefited from this rich revenue stream. However, once again circumstances intervened when Alexander died with his father on the field of Flodden.

This saga perfectly illustrates the connivance between Church and Crown in the appropriation of church revenues for purposes other than the promotion of the Gospel. From these machinations one can only conclude that from 1497 to 1513 Scotland's premier ecclesiastical office remained unoccupied by anyone qualified to provide appropriate leadership to the Scottish Church.

There were, of course, faithful priests quietly living out their calling and pressure for ecclesiastical reform was building. One of the issues the new Archbishop Blackadder had to deal with was a movement in Ayrshire that was challenging church teaching. Claims that the Pope was successor of Peter, the doctrine of purgatory, the worship of relics and the granting of indulgences were all dismissed by these radical thinkers. Known as 'the Lollards of Kyle', they not only rejected traditional practices; they positively affirmed counter-arguments in favour of the priesthood of all believers, the freedom of priests to marry (as distinct from turning a blind eye to concubinage) and the right of people to read the Bible in their own language. Such ideas were not particularly new. 'Lollardy' was the pejorative term (meaning 'mumbling') used to describe the teaching of the fourteenth-century English theologian, John Wycliffe. In Scotland it had already produced martyrs such as an Englishman, James Resby, burned at the stake in Perth in 1407, and a Bohemian, Paul Crawer, who suffered the same fate in St Andrews in 1433. In 1411 Laurence of Lindores, Abbot of Scone, had been appointed Inquisitor, charged with rooting out the heresy, and in 1416 the University of St Andrews decreed that applicants for the Master of Arts degree take an oath that they would resist all adherents of the sect of Lollards. The Kyle Lollards investigated by Bishop Blackadder were fortunate compared with Resby and Crawer. For all his abuse of church offices and revenues, James IV was a man of intelligence and ideas. He spoke several languages, encouraged poets such as William Dunbar and Robert Henryson and was instrumental in the establishment of Scotland's third university at Aberdeen. When the Ayr Lollards appeared before him he was inclined to leniency. A clue as to why may be found in a comment of John Knox. In his *History of the Reformation* he suggests that some of them were the king's 'great familiaris'.

Politically James' Scotland found itself in a triangular relationship with France (the Auld Alliance) and England (the Auld Enemy). This created tensions that in the 1490s led to military campaigns against England; though things looked more settled when, in 1502, a Treaty of Perpetual Peace with England was signed. One of the fruits of this was James' marriage to Margaret Tudor, daughter of Henry VII of England. Nevertheless, old habits die hard, and when war broke out between England and France, James supported France. War was declared on England, and the Scottish fleet, a significant naval force, was dispatched to support the French. By this time James' brother-in-law had succeeded to the English throne as Henry VIII. Aware that Henry was in France with his forces, James saw his opportunity, led an army south and engaged the English at Flodden. The disastrous outcome was a wiping out of the 'flower of Scotland' and the bringing to the throne of James' son aged just seventeen months. James IV, who twenty-five years earlier had come to the throne on the field of battle, left it in the same way.

THE SIXTEENTH CENTURY

Martin Luther's Ninety-Five Theses

According to tradition, on 31 October 1517, Martin Luther nailed his Ninety-Five Theses to the door of All Saints Church in Wittenberg. It was an event that sent shockwaves across Europe and gave a huge impetus to the demand for religious reform.

Luther was born into a mining family at Eisleben, Germany, in 1483. In 1501 he entered the University of Erfurt, graduating with a Master's degree in 1505. At his father's behest he proceeded to study law but soon dropped out, being drawn instead to the study of theology. The story is told that on a visit home he was caught in a fierce storm and prayed to St Anna, patron saint of miners, promising to enter a monastery if she would save him. In that same year he was admitted to a closed Augustinian friary in Erfurt and began to submit himself to the life and discipline of a monk. His father was unimpressed, regarding this as a waste of a good education. Two years later Luther was ordained as a priest and in 1508 was invited to teach theology at the recently established University of Wittenberg. In 1512 he was awarded the degree of Doctor of Theology and admitted to the Senate of the University.

At this time a major project was the rebuilding of St Peter's in Rome, and a rich source of funding was the selling of indulgences to the faithful. These purported to offer forgiveness of sins and shorten the period the purchaser might have to spend in Purgatory after death. This flew in the face of what Luther's studies had led him to believe, particularly from Paul's letter to the Romans; namely that people could be saved only by divine grace mediated through faith in Jesus Christ. Salvation was not something that could be purchased like a commodity or a reward for good deeds. For Luther this was a profound revelation, a defining moment, and it moved him to write a letter of protest to his bishop. Enclosed with the letter was a document entitled 'Disputation of Martin Luther on the Power and Efficacy of Indulgences'. This became known as 'The Ninety-Five Theses'. It is now reckoned that Luther was not seeking a public confrontation, rather a theological debate on the nature of faith and salvation. Be that as it may, there was no doubting the force of his questioning of the Church's teaching and practice. One of the theses asked why the Pope, 'whose wealth today is greater than the wealth of the richest Crassus, builds the basilica of St Peter with the money of poor believers rather than his own money'. Such a challenge could not be ignored and it wasn't. Indeed, it had the twofold effect of galvanising those who wished to see the Church reformed and mobilising upholders and beneficiaries of the policy to rally to the Church's defence.

Particularly helpful in spreading the call for reform was the recently invented printing press, and Luther made full use of it. Indeed, it has been calculated that he was responsible for 20 per cent of the output of German printing presses between 1500 and 1530, a flow that vastly exceeded that of his antagonists. The Theses spread rapidly across Europe, eventually reaching Scotland through travellers from the continent who had embraced this new theological thinking. Their arrival inspired those in Scotland who shared Luther's concerns, including Patrick Hamilton and George Wishart.

It was in 1523 that the nineteen-year-old Patrick Hamilton began his studies at St Andrews University. Hamilton was extremely well connected, his father being Sir Patrick Hamilton of Kincavil and his mother Catherine Stewart, a granddaughter of James III. In 1517 the thirteen-year-old Hamilton was appointed titular abbot of Fearn Abbey and the proceeds of the benefice paid for his education. This is somewhat ironic given that such appropriation of ecclesiastical revenues by the nobility was one of the main grievances of the Reformers.

Four days before Hamilton's arrival in St Andrews, James Beaton had been installed as archbishop. As Lord Chancellor, Beaton was already Scotland's leading statesman. He now became its leading churchman as well. In 1525 Parliament passed an Act against Lutheranism and this gave Beaton his opportunity. The heresy hunt was on and Patrick Hamilton, who had generally kept his head down, was summoned to answer a charge of spreading Lutheran ideas. Sensing a trap, Hamilton left Scotland and travelled to Germany where he enrolled at the University of Marburg. While there he published his own 'Theses', which became known as 'Patrick's Places'. In these he set out 'commonplaces' of the Reformed Faith, centred round Luther's core doctrine of justification by faith. In 1527 he returned to Scotland, began to preach and soon found himself invited to confer with Beaton. This time he accepted, returned to St Andrews and participated in a series of colloquies. It transpired, however, that this apparently civilised dialogue was no more than a ruse to lead Hamilton to incriminate himself. The mood changed and he was summoned to answer a charge of heresy. Once again friends urged him to flee, but he refused. There are suggestions that Beaton himself would have been content not to press things to their inevitable conclusion. Given Hamilton's royal pedigree this is understandable; but the die was cast. The trial went ahead with Hamilton effectively pleading guilty as charged. The outcome was inevitable. The accused was declared to be a heretic, guilty of 'disputing, holding and maintaining divers heresies of Martin Luther and his followers'. The very same day, 29 February 1528, Hamilton was burned at the stake at the entrance to St Salvator's College. It was a particularly horrific event. The day was wet, the wood was damp and it reportedly took six hours to finish the job. The location is marked by the initials 'PH' laid into the cobbled pavement. To this day respectful St Andrews students maintain a tradition of never walking on them, and tour guides point to the image of a human face in the stonework above the arched entrance to the quadrangle. Some say it was scorched into the tower by the bright face of an angel sent to comfort the martyr; others suggest it was caused by a beatific radiance from Hamilton's own face as he died for his faith.

Reaction to these proceedings was the precise opposite of what Beaton intended. The Reformation cause was given a great boost as, in the words of John Lindsay, one of Beaton's advisers: 'My Lord, if you burn any more, let it be in underground cellars, for the reek of Master Patrick Hamilton has infected as many as it blew upon.'

James V – Solway Moss

When James IV was killed at Flodden the throne passed to his infant son. Less than two weeks after the battle, on 21 September 1513, he was crowned James V at Stirling Castle. Initially his mother, Margaret Tudor, sister of Henry VIII, ruled as Regent, but on her remarriage the following year to the Earl of Angus, the Regency passed to the Duke of Albany. As a grandson of James II and cousin of James IV he was next in line to the throne after the young king. The Queen Mother and her husband did not take kindly to this new arrangement and tensions simmered, leading to factions within the national leadership. Not until 1528, aged sixteen, did James assume personal rule when, once again, the great issue of the day was whether Scotland should align with France or with England.

When in 1534 Henry VIII finally broke with Rome he put pressure on his Scottish nephew to follow suit. James resisted, yielding rather to persuasion by the King of France and the Pope. One of James' chief advisers at the time was David Beaton, nephew of James Beaton and, like his uncle, a leading figure in both Church and State. In time he would succeed his uncle as Archbishop of St Andrews and wear a cardinal's hat. Under

Beaton's influence James remained loyal to the Catholic Church and allied to France. He married Madeleine, a daughter of the French King François I, and, following her untimely death, he looked again to France, marrying Mary of Guise, of the House of Lorraine. It is not coincidental that at this time the French king nominated Beaton for the lucrative French bishopric of Mirepoix. However, such Francophile/Catholic supporting policies served only to stiffen the resolve of those seeking reform. The late fifteenth-century struggle over rank between Schevez and Blackadder continued anew between Beaton and his opposite number at Glasgow, Gavin Dunbar. A particularly scandalous incident occurred in Glasgow Cathedral in 1545 when an argument over precedence in a procession culminated in 'fisticuffs' between the prelates and their supporters.

Alongside his twin loyalty to the Catholic Church and the French alliance, James sought to keep the senior clergy on their toes by hinting that he might introduce his Uncle Henry's reforms into Scotland. He encouraged writers such as the satirist Sir David Lindsay and appointed the learned Protestant sympathiser, George Buchanan, as tutor to one of his sons. At the same time Parliament passed a series of Acts, one of which was entitled 'for reforming of Kirkis and Kirkmen'. This directly impugned the 'unhonestie and misreule of kirkmen' and identified these failings as the cause of low esteem in which church leaders were held. The Act went on to urge archbishops, prelates and churchmen generally 'to reform thare selfis and kirkmen under thame in habit and maneris to God and man'. Cardinal Beaton, along with other senior clergy, was present when Parliament passed this legislation, yet there was no follow-up, no ecclesiastical council held to begin a process of reform. Indeed, shortly afterwards Beaton travelled to France on a diplomatic mission to cement relations and seek a wider alliance against Henry's England. One outcome was the arrangement of a 'summit meeting' between James and Henry, to be held at York. James, perhaps playing for time, wished the meeting to be deferred until his queen had given birth to the child she was carrying. He was also alert to rumours that he might be kidnapped by the English king. The request for a delay was rejected but James still failed to appear. Henry was furious, deeming his nephew's behaviour not just as rank discourtesy, but as clear evidence of the Scots' commitment to an alliance with Catholic France rather than Protestant England. The time for talking was over and hostilities should resume.

As it happened, Henry's sister, James' mother, had died earlier that year (1542), severing a personal and familial tie between Scotland and England. Learning of Henry's plans James, against the advice of his generals, decided to get his retaliation in first. A Scots raiding party entered England and attacked an English force at Solway Moss in Cumberland. The outcome was an ignominious defeat for the Scots. James did not take part in the battle, but within a fortnight he was dead. As the thirty-one-year-old king lay dying at Falkland Palace his wife gave birth to a little girl. On being informed James is said to have murmured, referring to the Stewart dynasty: 'it cam wi' a lass and it'll gang wi' a lass'. The reference was to the beginnings of the Stewart line through Marjorie Bruce. Within a few days the lass became James' infant heir. We know her as Mary Queen of Scots.

For the second time in thirty years Scotland was vulnerable to an English military move. The Franco-Scottish alliance was holding and tensions between England and France were running high. Back in 1513 both Scotland and England had been within the Catholic fold but by the time of Solway Moss, England had shifted its religious alignment. Henry wished Scotland to follow the same path and with this strategy in mind he pursued three tactics. The first of these involved taking prisoner many prominent Scots who had been captured after Solway Moss. These were subsequently and gradually released on condition that they would return home and make the case for a strong alliance with England. Second, he encouraged the export of Protestant tracts in the hope of destabilising the Scots' Catholic allegiance. Third, he proposed a dynastic marriage between his son and heir Edward and the young Scots Queen Mary.

Following James V's death the immediate question for the Scottish political establishment had been the appointment of a Regent to act on behalf of the infant queen. Cardinal Beaton wasted no time in producing a document, asserting that it had been signed by the dying king, appointing him to discharge this high office. This was suspected to be a forgery, Beaton was imprisoned and a meeting of nobles was called to resolve the matter. They convened on New Year's Day, 1543 and their choice was James Hamilton, Earl of Arran, a great-grandson of James II and heir-presumptive to the throne. At the time Arran was sympathetic to the Reform cause and appointed like-minded chaplains to preach at Holyrood and St Giles. A Parliament was called and met on 12 March that year. Ambassadors from England were present to press the case for the marriage between Mary and Edward that Henry desired. Parliament also passed an Act authorising the reading of the Bible in the language of the people. This was certainly in line with Arran's sympathies at the time, but it is interesting to note that the proposal came from Lord Maxwell, one of the returned prisoners following Solway Moss. Henry would have approved, but the Scottish clergy did not. Archbishop Gavin Dunbar of Glasgow recorded his dissent and a compromise was agreed. This restricted popular access to the Bible simply to reading; follow-up discussion was firmly forbidden. However, any victory for Reform was short-lived. Beaton was eventually released from prison and this led to a concerted push against the Regent's English/Reform policy and in favour the French/Catholic connection. In June a proclamation banned the possession of 'heretical' books and forbad criticism of the Sacraments. In September, Regent Arran, a notorious trimmer, repented publicly of his 'apostasy' and was granted absolution by Beaton. The following day, 9 September, the infant Mary was crowned at Stirling Castle. On 3 December Parliament met and revoked the royal marriage treaty between

Mary and Edward agreed just six months earlier. The French alliance was reaffirmed and further laws passed against the spreading of 'heresy'. For good measure Beaton was made Chancellor of Scotland.

With the coming of spring, Henry began his fight back and there commenced the 'rough wooing', in response to the rejection of his desired marriage treaty between Edward and Mary. On 3 May an English fleet of 300 ships and 10,000 men entered the Forth, taking Leith and sacking and burning their way into Edinburgh itself. Meanwhile, an invading army had made its way north to join the fray, doing much damage on the way. The evidence remains to this day in the ruined abbeys of Melrose, Jedburgh, Kelso and Dryburgh – the destruction caused by the invading English forces not, as is sometimes suggested, by Protestant iconoclasts.

It was around this time that another significant figure was to emerge. George Wishart was an Angus man, educated at the new University of Aberdeen and a teacher in the grammar school at Montrose. In 1535 he came to the attention of the Bishop of Brechin for teaching his pupils to read the Greek New Testament. Sensing danger, he left Scotland for Bristol, thence to Switzerland, where he came into contact with the Reform movement in that country. From Switzerland Wishart returned to England, where he was appointed a tutor at Corpus Christi College, Cambridge. In 1543 he made his way back to Scotland and began teaching and preaching in accordance with the reformed faith. He spent time in Ayrshire, where he had strong support from the continuing Lollard tradition. From there he moved east, being particularly drawn to Dundee at a time of plague and great suffering in that city. His next move was to prove fateful. At Ormiston in East Lothian he was arrested and delivered into the hands of Cardinal Beaton. On 1 March 1546, at St Andrews, he was condemned as a heretic and then, in John Knox's words, 'put upon a gibbet and hanged, and then burnt to powder'.

Meanwhile, the threat from the south continued and in 1547 English forces gained a significant victory at the Battle of Pinkie, near Musselburgh. Henry had died in January of that year and the ten-year-old Edward VI reigned in his place. Mary, his no-longer intended bride, now four years old, was being brought up by her mother, Mary of Guise. The safety of the young queen was clearly a concern. Her father's death meant that any prospect of a 'spare' had gone, leaving Mary as his sole dynastic heir. The Scots defeat at Pinkie further underlined the fragility of the situation and it would have come as very welcome news to Mary of Guise when Henri II of France proposed a marriage between her daughter and his son and heir, the Dauphin François. Henri, aware of young Mary's vulnerability and conscious also that, through marriage to his son, she could one day be Queen of France, pressed for her to be brought up at the French court. There was Scottish resistance to this, including from the Regent Arran. However, this was overcome, perhaps not entirely coincidentally, when the French king granted Arran the French dukedom of Châtellherault. Accordingly, in June 1548 the young queen set sail for France, leaving behind her mother, who remained dutifully at her post and who, five years later, would replace Arran as Regent.

John Knox

The name of John Knox has been mentioned once or twice in passing. It is now time to introduce him more substantially to the narrative. Along with Patrick Hamilton and George Wishart he is a towering figure in the story of the Scottish Reformation. Hamilton and Wishart gave their lives to the cause; Knox survived not only to make it happen but to see it prevail.

He was born in Haddington around 1515 and educated at the local grammar school. From there he proceeded to St Andrews University to study under John Major, one of the great scholars of the age. A 1540 record describes him both as priest

*Statue of John Knox
in St Giles' Cathedral.*

Copyright © Peter Backhouse

and notary and a 1543 reference describes him as 'a minister
of the sacred altar in the diocese of St Andrews, notary by
apostolic authority'. He did not immediately take up a parochial
appointment but was appointed tutor to the sons of Hugh
Douglas, Laird of Longniddry, and to the son of John Cockburn
of Ormiston – both in East Lothian. As previously noted, it was
at Ormiston that George Wishart had been arrested and taken
to St Andrews for trial and execution. In fact Knox was not only
a disciple of Wishart; he was his bodyguard and sword-bearer.
He had been present when Wishart was taken and was minded
to stand by him. Wishart, however, dissuaded him, allegedly
remarking that 'one is sufficient for a sacrifice'. Recognising
the force of this, Knox remained in East Lothian as tutor to the
Douglas and Cockburn boys. Events then moved dramatically
and on 29 May, in a daring and carefully planned raid on the

castle at St Andrews, Cardinal Beaton was murdered. Under cover of building work, the assassins had entered and taken possession of the castle. Beaton was stabbed to death in his chamber and, for good measure, his body hung from a window as proof of the deed. Given Beaton's role, not only as high-ranking ecclesiastic but also leading statesman and champion of the French-Catholic alliance, his assassination was not simply a revenge killing, though it certainly was that, but also a *coup d'état.*

The safest course for the assassins was to remain within the castle, where they were soon joined by others to a number of around 150. They had a useful asset in that the young son of the Regent Arran was a member of Beaton's household. In fact he had been placed there by Beaton as a hostage for the Regent's good behaviour (in Beaton's view) but now became a different kind of hostage, and certainly a useful one. Obviously there was satisfaction among those seeking reform. At the same time there was an ugly mood among many, for Beaton had been a strong man who had stood up to the forceful Henry VIII. The siege dragged on for many months, despite Arran raising an army to end it. In the December, seven months after the assassination, a truce of sorts was brokered, which allowed the 'Castilians', as they became known, to remain, pending an absolution from the Pope. On receipt of that they were to surrender without suffering any penalty. In January 1547 Henry VIII died, and in the April of that same year John Knox himself sought refuge in the castle, accompanied by his young East Lothian charges, at the request of their parents.

During this period of stalemate, those holding the castle had a fair degree of freedom to move around the town. While John Hamilton, a half-brother of the Regent, had been appointed Beaton's successor as archbishop, he had not yet taken up the role. Meantime, the administration of the archdiocese was in the hands of the Vicar General, John Winram. Winram was one of those who remained loyal to the Church but who also acknowledged the case for reform. Controversially, he agreed that Knox could preach in the parish church, though only on weekdays. The concession was one of which Knox took full opportunity.

Meantime, Arran and Mary of Guise were seeking help from France to end the siege. Eventually, at the end of June, a fleet of ships carrying a significant force arrived in St Andrews Bay. Arran justified involving the French on the grounds that the Castilians had received the promised papal pardon, but rejected it as irrelevant. In the same way they now rejected the French command to surrender. Another stand-off ensued, broken eventually at the end of July, when Arran arrived with an army, and a combined assault from land and sea finally ended the siege. All lives were to be spared but under a condition that they were transported to France from where they would be free to move on, anywhere but back to Scotland. Knox fared less well. Given his role as teacher and preacher of 'heretical' views he was made a galley slave, a role he endured for nineteen months. From his *History of the Reformation in Scotland* comes a story of his galley passing between Dundee and St Andrews in the summer of 1548. The spire of the parish church appeared in the distance and a fellow prisoner asked Knox if he recognised it. He replied that indeed he did. It was where he had first preached; adding that he would preach there again before he died. Eventually Knox was released in February 1549, and decided to seek sanctuary in England. He was licensed to preach in the Church of England in April of that year and appointed to minister in Berwick. It was while there that he met his future wife, Marjorie Bowes. Her father, a staunch Catholic, opposed the match but her mother, Elizabeth, was to become a great supporter.

In June of that same year, 1549, Cardinal Beaton's successor, John Hamilton, was finally enthroned as Archbishop of St Andrews. One of his first actions was to call a Provincial Council at Linlithgow, and this was followed over the next decade by further Councils. While loyal to the Catholic Church

Hamilton was not insensitive to the need for reform. Issues such as clergy immorality and the general ignorance of the laity, and of some clergy as well, could not continue to be tolerated. To the extent that these gatherings in Council involved both traditional and reform-minded churchmen they offered an opportunity for seeking a resolution of the growing crisis. Inevitably, though, an easier target was those deemed to be promulgating heretical views, and many thought the elimination of such dissent was the real priority. In any event, there was little evidence of commitment to real reform of clerical morals or a directing of the Church's financial resources towards work at parish level. Indeed, this question went to the heart of the matter. For decades ecclesiastical wealth had funded the higher echelons of the Church, not to mention the royal household, and there was neither incentive nor effective pressure for this to change.

In the end something positive did emerge from a Provincial Council of 1552. This was a document that became known as 'Hamilton's Catechism'. Essentially, it was an exposition of the faith that was to be read in churches on Sundays when there was no preacher. No discussion of the document was to be allowed, but one striking omission from the text was any reference to the authority of the Pope. Was this a gesture to those urging reform? Given the concern over lay and clerical ignorance, the 'Catechism' was a logical development, and the fact that no discussion was to be allowed perhaps reflected a concern that many priests would be unable to answer any questions raised. The authorship is unknown but it has been conjectured that it was the work of John Winram.

In 1551 Knox took up a ministry in Newcastle and was appointed a chaplain to King Edward VI. Two years later he was invited to London to preach before the royal court, where he used the opportunity to argue against the English practice of kneeling to receive communion. This led to a debate in which Cranmer, Archbishop of Canterbury, defended the custom. A compromise agreement resulted in the practice continuing, but with a printed rubric added to the liturgy explaining that kneeling merely signified a 'humble and grateful acknowledging of the benefits of Christ given to the worthy receiver'. In other words, it did not imply any adoration of the bread and wine or the real presence of Christ's flesh and blood. This victory added value to Knox's stock. He had already made an impression on John Dudley, Duke of Northumberland, who had been appointed Regent during Edward's minority. Dudley had heard Knox preach in Newcastle and now invited him to become Bishop of Rochester. Knox, however, declined, wishing to return to Newcastle and remain nearer to Scotland. The following year (1553) he was again invited to London to preach before the king, and this time was offered the appointment of Vicar of All Hallows Church in the English capital. He duly preached before the court but, as in the case of Rochester, declined the All Hallows position. He did, however, accept an appointment to Amersham in Buckinghamshire, where he remained for a few months. Then, on 6 July, everything changed. Edward VI, whose health had been deteriorating, died and his half-sister, Mary Tudor ('Bloody Mary'), came to the throne. Six months later, in January 1554, Knox left England for Geneva, where he remained for some months in the company of John Calvin and other reformers. He also travelled to Zurich and Basel.

John Calvin

Calvin was born at Noyon in Picardy on 10 July 1509. That made him six years older than Knox and twenty-six years younger than Luther. He was a clever child and his education was funded by his appointment, aged twelve, to a chaplaincy in the cathedral at Noyon. This financially beneficial sinecure, which has echoes of Patrick Hamilton at Fearn Abbey, was arranged by his father, a lay administrator to the bishop. Two years later, again under the influence of his father, the young Calvin enrolled at the University of Paris to begin training for the priesthood. After four years, however, Calvin senior had a change of mind and directed his son to the study of law at Orleans, subsequently at Bourges.

In 1531, following the death of his father, Calvin returned to Paris. There his studies included Latin, Greek and Hebrew, which enabled him to read the Scriptures in their original languages. At Paris he also came under the influence of Protestant scholars and eventually abandoned the Catholicism in which he had been nurtured. This was a potentially dangerous move and in 1533 he left Paris and returned to Noyon, where he formally resigned the cathedral chaplaincy. The following year, due to an upsurge of anti-Protestant violence, he thought it prudent to move to Basel in Switzerland and there, in 1536, he published the first edition of *The Institutes of the Christian Religion*. This was a systematic exposition of Protestant Christianity, which he was to develop and expand through several editions. It remains a definitive text to this day. From Basel he moved to Ferrara in northern Italy before deciding to settle in Strasbourg. His route took him through Geneva, but his onward journey was delayed due to roads being blocked by military manoeuvres. Geneva had only recently embraced the Reformation and the pastor there was William Farel. On learning that Calvin was in the city he invited him to stay and share in his ministry. Calvin, intent on a quiet life of study and writing in Strasbourg, initially resisted but Farel refused to take 'No' for an answer and eventually prevailed.

Calvin was a second-generation Reformer who thought that, in some respects, Luther had not gone far enough. While accepting Luther's view that the individual was saved by faith, as distinct from good deeds, he also recognised that the Christian life called for behaviour rooted in the teachings of the Bible. Accordingly, what he and Farel sought was a community of godly people whose way of life reflected the values of their Christian faith. To this end Farel prepared a Confession of Faith to which citizens were expected to subscribe, while Calvin drafted Articles for regulating the life and worship of the Church.

These texts set out the theory, but the practical establishment of such a community also required discipline; and the exercise of discipline called for sanctions. This is where the plan started to break down. Not everyone was willing to sign the Confession and then tensions began to emerge between the Reforming ministers and the City Council. For example, the Council demanded a role in cases of excommunication where sentence carried civil consequences, but Calvin and Farel refused. There was also trouble when the Council instructed that unleavened bread be used for the Easter communion services, as was the practice in Bern. The ministers' reaction was to refuse to celebrate the Sacrament altogether. This provoked a riot and they were expelled from the city. Farel moved to Neuchâtel and Calvin reverted to his original plan and travelled to Strasbourg, where for the next three years he ministered to French Protestant refugees.

In 1541 there was a change of regime in Geneva and Calvin was invited to return and resume his ministry. In this (for him) more congenial climate, new powers were given to the clergy to instruct and admonish the populace, in public and in private, all with a view to exercising 'fraternal correction'. Using these powers, Calvin resumed his project of establishing a society where good works abounded as evidence that the people were living out the Gospel. While this might sound idyllic, the reality was rather different. There were regulations governing all aspects of life, from style of dress to the naming children. Biblical names were particularly encouraged and a minister might well decline to baptise a child if he disapproved of the name. Even the naming of pets was monitored and the naming of a dog 'Calvin' was not a cause of ecclesiastical amusement. Innkeepers were expected to ensure there was no dancing or playing at cards, and guests were to be in bed by 9 p.m. Only informers were permitted to stay up later than that. A Consistory Court was established to judge alleged misconduct and determine punishments. The emphasis was on a reform of behaviour, and those making a first appearance were treated less severely than persistent offenders. The Consistory took a particularly stern view of offences such as witchcraft, blasphemy and heresy, and more severe sentences included fines and imprisonment. Banishment was also an option, and even execution, for offences judged the most extreme.

One matter of debate among the Reformers was the nature of Christ's presence in the Eucharist. Catholic teaching was clear enough. The doctrine of transubstantiation taught that when the priest consecrated the bread and wine these miraculously became the body and blood of Christ. Luther rejected this but, in its place, offered a theory known as 'consubstantiation' (though Luther himself did not use the term). While rejecting transubstantiation, this theory still averred a 'real presence' whereby, on consecration, the inner substance of Christ's body and blood were mysteriously joined with that of the bread and wine.

Calvin also affirmed the presence of Christ in the Sacrament, but for him it was a spiritual presence. He held that those who received the bread and wine in faith were, through the power of the Holy Spirit, nourished by the body and blood of Christ. The classic definition, deriving from Augustine, is that a Sacrament is a visible sign of an invisible grace. Following this Calvin expressed the matter thus: 'For why does the Lord put the symbol of his body into your hands, but just to assure you that you truly partake of him.' It was this understanding that would find expression in the *Scots Confession* of 1560, which we shall come to in due course.

A particular objection of the Reformers to the doctrine of transubstantiation was the notion of a priest offering Christ's body and blood as a sacrificial offering on behalf of the people. Did this not imply that the original sacrifice of Calvary needed to be repeated over and over again? By contrast, the Reformed view was that Christ had died once and for all and the basis of the Sacrament was his command: 'this do in remembrance of me'. The Sacrament was instituted at the Last Supper, but in all likelihood its next celebration was at Emmaus, where the risen Lord was known in the breaking of bread. Thereafter, the breaking of bread formed part of the regular Sunday worship of the infant Church. The Eucharist thus commemorates and celebrates the crucified and risen Christ. It is also of interest to note that Calvin favoured a weekly celebration of Holy Communion.

While Calvin never visited Scotland his influence on the shape of the Scottish Reformation was profound. Knox was a disciple and the two men were close, and when Knox's first wife died in December 1560, Calvin (himself by then a widower) was deeply concerned and wrote to Knox describing Marjorie as 'the most delightful of wives'. Indeed, he would have known the whole family, as John and Marjorie's sons were born during their time in Geneva and given the appropriately biblical names of Nathaniel and Eleazar.

Frankfurt, Geneva, Scotland and the Monstrous Regiment

We meet up again with John Knox nine months after he had left England for Geneva. In September 1554 he accepted an invitation to minister to a congregation of English exiles in Frankfurt. This was not a happy move. New groups of refugees from Mary Tudor's England kept arriving, with strong leaders of some seniority. These held determined and divergent views on forms of service, including some who supported kneeling to receive communion. Inevitably, Knox became embroiled in endless arguments, with the consequence that, following some deft politicking by opponents, he found himself expelled from the city. This was just six months after he had arrived. Shaking the dust from his shoes he returned to Geneva and took up a ministry there. However, in August 1555, prompted by a letter from Elizabeth Bowes, he decided to return to Scotland. He arrived in Berwick, where he and Marjorie Bowes became betrothed. Thereafter he continued his journey north.

Back in Scotland, Knox was much encouraged by what he saw. He was free to travel and preach and was generally well received. A network of 'privy kirks' was developing through which reform-minded individuals met in homes for worship and religious discussion. Supporting these gatherings was an emerging organisation of elders, deacons, preachers and readers of Scripture who were assigned various tasks. Knox preached at such meetings and celebrated the Sacrament of the Lord's Supper. He also sought to curb a practice that was known as 'Nicodemism', namely, embracing the Reform cause in private while adhering to the Catholic Church in public. The term derives from Nicodemus, the Pharisee who came secretly to Jesus by night. The nobles who were supporting reform judged it important to retain the favour of Mary of Guise, who was by this time Regent, and one sure way of doing this was to continue attending Mass. This they judged both politic and diplomatic, though Knox would have none of it. The Regent was also being diplomatic in not seeking to interfere with Knox's activities, but the Scottish bishops viewed him as a threat and summoned him to appear before them. Knox duly complied but when he appeared, accompanied by a large number of highly influential supporters, the hearing was abandoned. Meanwhile, he continued to preach in Edinburgh with much success, prompting two prominent men, the Earl of Glencairn and Earl Marshall William Keith, to persuade him to write a tactful letter to Mary of Guise. Doubtless Glencairn and Keith had been encouraged by the Regent's tolerance of Knox's preaching. Tactful letters were not Knox's strong suit but eventually the epistle, urging her to support church reform, was composed and delivered. The letter went unacknowledged, but word filtered out that Mary had thought the whole thing a huge joke. She referred to Knox's letter as a 'pasquil' (satire) and passed it round her courtiers, including the Archbishop of Glasgow, amid much hilarity.

In November 1555 the Geneva congregation invited Knox

to be their minister and, judging that the time was not ripe for a final push in Scotland, he accepted the call. Before setting off it is thought that his betrothal to Marjorie became a formal marriage, as she and her mother accompanied him. This left the leadership of the Reform movement in the hands of a younger group of nobles who banded together to advance the cause. This alliance became labelled the 'First Band' and represented a growing confidence and solidarity. With Knox out of the way and encouraged no doubt by the Regent's response to his tactful letter, the church hierarchy counter-attacked, condemning Knox and having his effigy burned in Edinburgh.

This next sojourn in Geneva was to be one of the happiest periods of Knox's life. In a letter to friends in England he described the city as 'the most perfect school of Christ that ever was in the earth since the days of the apostles', though not all residents, particularly those subject to Calvin's disciplinary regime, would have shared that assessment. He preached regularly in the church known today as the Auditoire de Calvin, and it was during this sojourn that he and Marjorie were blessed with the birth of their two sons. However, this peaceful interlude was rudely interrupted in May 1557 when visitors from Scotland arrived with a message that the time was now right for him to return home. At a personal level this was not what he wanted to hear, but he could hardly refuse the request. Nevertheless, it was not until the October that he set off on the long overland journey to Dieppe. Imagine, then, his irritation on arriving there to find a letter advising that the time was not as ripe as previously reported.

Much was certainly going on in Scotland, including finalisation of arrangements for the young Queen Mary to marry the Dauphin, though this was not being met with universal acclaim. One major concern was that Mary might grant her husband the crown matrimonial, thereby making him King of Scotland as well as of France. On top of this the Duke of Châtellherault (the former Regent Arran) had a more personal agenda. Were Mary to die he was next in line to the Scottish throne. After her marriage any children would push him down the line of succession. In addition, French pressure was being applied to Scottish nobles who had already declared for reform, with tempting inducements to re-establish the Auld Alliance and reconsider their religious allegiance. While all this was going on, Knox remained in France awaiting further word, before finally abandoning his visit and returning to Geneva.

In the summer of the following year (1558) he published what is probably his most infamous tract, *The First Blast of the Trumpet against the Monstrous Regiment of Women*. This was published anonymously, though the identity of the writer soon emerged. Possible misgivings on Knox's part might be inferred from the fact that, though drafting the document in Geneva, he did not consult Calvin on the matter. Was he concerned that Calvin might persuade him to think again? Did he think it was just another pamphlet and hardly worth troubling his chief with? The most common misunderstanding of *The First Blast* is to think that the word 'regiment' refers to a large and overbearing female crowd and assume that the pamphlet is simply a misogynist rant. In fact the word refers to the rule of women, and in the sixteenth century the word 'monstrous' indicated what we would describe today as 'unnatural'. The pamphlet was aimed principally at Mary Tudor, Queen of England and, to a lesser extent, Mary of Guise, Regent of Scotland. Both were Catholic and no friends of the Reformation.

Many today would agree that Mary Tudor's reign was monstrous (in the modern sense), justifying the title 'Bloody Mary'. But in the sense of 'unnatural' it should be recalled that in those days there was a natural presumption in favour of male rulers. This was why Henry VIII had successive wives and why Edward VI, the youngest of his children, succeeded ahead of his older half-sisters. To this extent, *The First Blast* might just have been another diatribe. The real problem, however, was that Knox didn't simply express opinions, albeit very colourfully; he actually went on to call for action, in particular for Mary Tudor, 'that cursed Jezebel of England', to be overthrown. To Knox this would have seemed the perfectly logical consequence of his argument. However, it was one thing to publish a polemical tract; quite another to urge regicide. Many Protestants thought he had gone too far, including Calvin, who disassociated himself from the document and banned its sale in Geneva.

With hindsight, *The First Blast* was a serious miscalculation. Of course, Knox could not have known that within months of its publication Mary Tudor would be dead and the Protestant Elizabeth on the throne. Unfortunately for him, she too had been deeply offended by the pamphlet. There were question marks anyway over her legitimacy. Henry VIII had married her mother, Anne Boleyn, while his first wife, Catherine of Aragon (Mary Tudor's mother), was still alive. In consequence, there was an argument that the rightful heir to the English throne was Mary, Queen of Scots, who was a thoroughly legitimate great-granddaughter of Henry VII. Given the future importance of the English alliance for the Scottish Reformation, this alienation of the English queen was not a smart move. An early indication of Elizabeth's displeasure came the following year. Knox decided to return to Scotland but had to make the long road and sea journey via Dieppe because Elizabeth refused him a safe passage through England.

The Final Push

On his eventual arrival in Scotland in 1559, Knox was declared an outlaw by Mary of Guise. However, this did not deter him from preaching to a large body of supporters in Perth. Rather pointedly the theme of his sermon, preached on 11 May in St John's Kirk, was the cleansing of the temple. Unfortunately things rather got out of hand and a riot ensued, with the smashing of images and the looting of friaries. The Regent, fearing civil war, dispatched the Earl of Argyll and Lord James Stewart to Perth to negotiate a re-establishment of order. However, contrary to assurances given to her emissaries, she decided to travel to Perth herself with armed support. The uneasy truce facilitated by the envoys was further undermined by her dismissal of the Protestant Lord Provost and a very pointed reinstating of the Mass. The result was that Argyll and Stewart felt betrayed and decided to join forces with the Reformers. In fact they went on to become leading members of a body known as 'the Lords of the Congregation' and played an important role in organising their peers and colleagues in the cause of reform. Knox, meantime, had moved on from Perth to St Andrews, perhaps recalling his earlier prophecy from the off-shore French galley. He did preach again in the parish church there, with consequences similar to those that attended his preaching in Perth.

As disorder spread through the central lowlands, the Regent travelled to Dunbar. Edinburgh itself was occupied at the end of June, with the inevitable sacking of churches and friaries. By the end of July, terms had been agreed that restored order to the city and allowed freedom of conscience in matters of religion. Suspecting that the Regent would seek military support from France, Knox made his way south to Northumberland and, using a pseudonym, sought negotiations with William Cecil, Secretary to Queen Elizabeth. No doubt the pseudonym was felt necessary after *The First Blast of the Trumpet*. Events were now moving quickly and a reinforcement of French troops arrived at Leith. The Scottish nobles responded by formally deposing Mary of Guise as Regent. Her Secretary, William Maitland, decided to join the Reformers and brought his considerable skills and experience with him. This freed Knox to concentrate solely on matters of religion. Meanwhile, negotiations with England proceeded, leading to the Treaty of Berwick, signed on 27 February 1560. This secured the support of English ships and troops for Scottish forces loyal to the Reformation and the eventual withdrawal of French troops from Scotland. On the night of 10/11 June, Mary of Guise died, and on 6 July the Treaty of Edinburgh was concluded. This provided for the withdrawal of all foreign troops from Scottish territory, the replacement of the Auld Alliance with a new Anglo-Scottish accord and a meeting of Parliament the following month. On 19 July, Knox led a national service of thanksgiving in St Giles'. Having preached in Perth a year earlier on the cleansing of the temple, he chose to preach on this occasion on the prophet Haggai's call to the returning exiles to rebuild the temple.

Over the previous year progress had certainly been gathering pace. In towns such as St Andrews, Ayr and Dundee, kirk sessions were functioning. The town council of Dundee had even passed an Act outlawing contempt of the Reformed Church and its officers, and in the early months of 1560 banns of marriage had been published in respect of some members of the clergy. In April the great Council of Scotland had instructed the ministers of Edinburgh to express their 'judgements touching the reformation of religion'. The resultant document became known as the 'Book of Common Reformation'. Certainly by the time Parliament met on 1 August, things were moving on the ground.

The Parliament was a well-attended gathering of Lords both temporal and spiritual, including the Catholic Primate, Archbishop Hamilton of St Andrews. The Bishops of Dunkeld and Dunblane were present and the case for reform was argued from within the Catholic establishment by John Winram, who had allowed Knox to preach in St Andrews. It is recorded that when Parliament was considering the Reformers' Confession of Faith (what we know as *The Scots Confession*), Archbishop Hamilton observed that 'as he would not utterly condemn it, so was he loth to give his consent thereto'. Unsurprisingly, Dunkeld and Dunblane concurred. There is, indeed, evidence that other bishops, not present, from dioceses as far apart as Galloway and Orkney had begun instituting reforming measures such as the abolition of the Latin rite and the institution of effective visitation. This both underlines the point that Reformation was a process as distinct from a moment in time, and that not all the Reformers were agitating Protestants. On 17 August, Parliament approved the *Confession of Faith*. A few days later it abolished the jurisdiction of the Pope and banned the saying or hearing of the Mass.

Notwithstanding such significant steps, the struggle was far from over. Archbishop Hamilton continued to preside at Mass without challenge and, later in the year, the Convention of Estates rejected proposals to divert the funds of the old Church to the support of the new. There was still some way to go. Moreover, questions were raised as to the regularity of these Parliamentary proceedings. The Treaty of Edinburgh had specifically precluded matters of religion from the Parliament's competence in the absence of the queen. There were also questions as to whether some of those present were legally eligible to take part. A fifteenth-century statute entitled lesser barons to attend Parliament, though for over a century none had done so; nevertheless, 110 turned up on this occasion. For several days before getting down to the real business, Parliament debated whether their right of attendance had fallen into desuetude. Finally, and potentially fatally, once legislation had been passed, no royal assent was given, as Mary Queen of Scots was still in France.

On the political and diplomatic front, the Auld Alliance with France was at an end but effective new connections remained to be established with England. The Tweed may no longer have represented a Catholic/Protestant border, but it still defined a national boundary. Yet another dynastic marriage was mooted between the son of the Earl of Arran and Queen Elizabeth of England. While Knox is reported to have favoured this plan, nothing came of it. Then, at the end of this momentous year, a quite unforeseen event occurred. The youthful François II, by then King of France, husband of Mary, Queen of Scots, died of an ear infection that had developed into an abscess of the brain. No longer Queen of France, did Mary's future now lie in Scotland? Commenting on her prospects, the Venetian ambassador observed: 'she has lost France and has little hope of Scotland'. How prophetic these words were to prove!

Securing the Reformation

While much remained unresolved, there was still scope for gains to be consolidated. Two major Reformation texts had been presented to the August 1560 Parliament, namely *The Scots Confession* and *The First Book of Discipline*. The first of these had been drawn up by six Johns: Knox, Winram, Spottiswoode, Willock, Douglas and Row. Knox, Willock and Spottiswoode were long-standing reformers; Winram, Douglas and Row had all held high office in the Catholic Church but had recognised the case for reform. According to tradition, the text, requested by Parliament for its consideration, had been drawn up in four days, under Knox's leadership. It was approved by Parliament as 'wholesome and sound doctrine grounded upon the infallible truth of God's word'. The Preface to the *Confession* asked: 'That if any man will note in this our Confession any article or sentence repugning to God's holy word, that it would please him of his gentleness and for Christian charity's sake to admonish us of the same in writing; and we do promise him satisfaction from the mouth of God, that it is from his holy Scriptures, or else reformation of that which he shall prove to be amiss.'

The same six Johns were also responsible for drawing up *The First Book of Discipline*. Essentially, this set out a shape and structure for a reformed Church. Two Sacraments only were identified: Baptism, which was to be administered in church in face of the congregation, and the Lord's Supper, which was to be celebrated quarterly, avoiding the old feast and saints' days of the Catholic Church. There was a strong focus on the ministry. Ministers were to be educated and possessed of 'giftis and graces able to edifie the Kirk of God'. Where a minister was not available, suitable persons were to be identified to fill the office of Reader. Their function was to read the Scriptures and prayers and, in the absence of a minister, to lead the service. As well as local ministers there were to be regional Superintendents covering ten districts, with responsibility for erecting churches and overseeing the work of the Church in their areas. This was a reduction of three on the number of pre-Reformation dioceses, and the aim was to ensure a ministerial presence throughout the country, not only in the main centres of population.

Alongside the question of manpower there was the matter of funding. As has already been seen, the pre-Reformation financial arrangements had involved lucrative Church benefices being used by the Crown to reward loyalty. Reclaiming such funds to support a nationwide structure of churches, ministers, poor relief and education was never going to be easy, and so it proved. The anomalous situation thus arose of a Protestant Church with her doctrine approved and acknowledged by Parliament as 'the only true and holy Kirk of Jesus Christ within this Realm', but unable to access the resources necessary for its work, locally and nationally.

Education was also addressed in *The First Book of Discipline*. What Knox and his colleagues proposed was nothing less than a whole system of elementary, secondary and higher education. Each parish would have its school, with secondary level provision in the larger towns, particularly the towns where superintendents were based. Responsibility for delivering this lofty aspiration would be willingly accepted by the Reformed Church and, once it received the patrimony of the pre-Reformation Church, those funds would be put to proper and worthy use. In truth though, as with the matter of financial support for the ministry, significant funding of such an educational vision was viewed by Parliament as 'devout imaginings'.

The penultimate section of *The First Book of Discipline* set out a scheme for electing elders and deacons, including a provision whereby elders could call the minister to account if they deemed him deserving of 'admonition'. Offences might include being 'licht in conversatioun, negligent in studie' or preaching 'not frutefull doctrine'. In theory this was a model of mutual responsibility. In practice it could readily lead to a complete breakdown in effective ministry within the parish. The final section addressed the religious education of the laity. In large towns there would be opportunities of daily preaching and prayer. In lesser towns that provision would be on one weekday as well as on Sunday. Each church would have a Bible in English and this would be read through and preached on systematically. Heads of households would accept responsibility for the religious knowledge of family members and servants.

A third significant Reformation document was the *Book of Common Order*. This originated in Geneva and was introduced in Scotland along with the English Book of Common Prayer. Indeed, there were many similarities in the patterns of Reformed worship north and south of the border. While Knox argued for quarterly communion, compared with Calvin's monthly celebration, the reality in many parts of pre-Reformation Scotland had been infrequent observance of the Mass. The basic order of Reformed worship included confession, psalms, Bible readings, sermon, intercessions, the Lord's Prayer and Apostles' Creed. In 1562, the General Assembly instructed that it be used for the administration of the Sacraments and in services for the solemnisation of marriage and burial of the dead. In 1564, a new and enlarged edition was printed in Edinburgh and the General Assembly instructed that every minister and reader should have a copy and use it in the leadership of worship.

It was January of 1561 before Parliament got round to considering the *First Book of Discipline*. As already noted the proposals to redistribute the resources that properly belonged to the Reformed Church were not acceptable to the nobles. The outcome was that two-thirds of the hoped-for funding was left in the hands of its existing owners, while the remaining third was to be shared between Church and the Crown. Right from the start the ambitious plans for education were hobbled, ministerial stipends were low and generally the Church found itself short-changed.

Notwithstanding such setbacks, the Reformed Church proceeded to make arrangements to fulfil its mission. A start was made to the appointing of superintendents, including some who had held office in the pre-Reformation Church. For example, John Winram was appointed Superintendent of Fife, Strathearn and Perthshire, and three former bishops who had accepted the Reformation were allowed to remain in their posts in Galloway, Orkney and Caithness. John Carswell, Superintendent of Argyll and the Isles, even published a Gaelic translation of the *Book of Common Order* for use in his vast and sparsely populated area. The vision was to staff over a thousand parishes with ministers, but progress was slow and not until 1574 was that number reached, many of these being drawn from the pre-Reformation priesthood.

In December 1560, continuing into January 1561, there was a gathering in Edinburgh of around forty people, comprising six ministers, along with lairds and civic representatives. This is regarded as the first General Assembly. Taking everything together, a structural pattern was beginning to emerge of local (minister and kirk session), regional (superintendents) and national (General Assembly).

Music and Song

An important legacy of the Scottish Reformation can be found in the metrical psalms, which enabled the people to add their voices to the congregation's songs of praise. By the Middle Ages, worship had largely become the preserve of the clergy and trained singers, who chanted the psalms, sang the anthems and contributed musical responses to the liturgy of the Mass. Bearing in mind that the spoken elements of the service would have been in Latin, the ordinary worshipper's role was passive in the extreme. A contemporary account of choral singing at the court of King David in twelfth-century Scotland is less than encouraging. It describes 'a-quavering like the neighing of horses' and refers to the singers 'with open mouths and their breath restrained as if they were expiring and not singing'. Things had improved considerably by the sixteenth century, thanks to the polyphonic music of composers such as Robert Johnson of Duns, Robert Douglas of Dunkeld and Robert Carver of Scone. It is also relevant to note that the martyred Patrick Hamilton had composed a Mass for Nine Voices, which had been sung under his direction in St Andrews Cathedral. Even so, such music, for all its undoubted enrichment of an act of worship, is hardly designed for congregational singing.

Martin Luther appreciated music and believed strongly in congregational singing. He wrote and encouraged what he called 'spiritual songs, whereby the Word of God may be kept alive among the people by singing'. The process was quite simple, namely verses in a regular metre set to easily learned tunes. In the early 1540s three Dundonian brother by the name of Wedderburn published *Ane Compendious Buik of Godlie Psalms and Spirituall Sangis, collectit furthe of sundrie partes of the Scripture*. These 'Good and Godly Ballads', as they came to be known, offered twenty-two psalm portions for the people to sing in their own Scots language. In his *History of the Reformation*, Knox has George Wishart singing one of the Wedderburn psalms on the night of his arrest at Ormiston. Indeed, such was their popularity and reforming influence that a 1543 Act of the Privy Council described them as 'slanderous Ballatis'. Calvin also recognised the value of congregational singing and introduced psalm arrangements to Strasbourg and Geneva. Some tunes from the period remain popular today. Examples include Old Hundredth, Martyrs, French, Winchester and Dunfermline. In 1564 the first Scottish Psalter appeared, drawing on English and continental predecessors but also including some original Scottish contributions.

While such an approach may be viewed as a positive step

there is another perspective, namely that it came at the price of extinguishing the rich choral tradition that had gone before. Organs were removed from churches and composers such as Robert Carver of Scone were not going to find any demand for their rich Mass settings. Indeed, it was not until the late twentieth century, thanks to the reconstructive work on ancient manuscripts carried out principally by Kenneth Elliot and the writing and broadcasting projects led by John Purser, that such music began to be heard again with any frequency. A memorable event during Glasgow's year as European City of Culture (1990) was the series of performances by Cappella Nova in Glasgow Cathedral of all five authenticated Carver Mass settings, possibly the first since the Reformation; certainly the first in quasi-liturgical format complete with plainchant Propers.

Concern at the threat to musical creativity was registered at the time. In 1579 the Scottish Parliament passed an Act for the instructing of the youth in music, responsibility for this being laid upon burgh councils. This enabled the restoration of pre-Reformation Sang Schules, the function of which had been to train choristers. Edward Henderson, the pre-Reformation master of the Sang Schule at St Giles', was continued in his role 'to learn the town's bairns in the art of music' so that they could lead the singing of the psalms on Sundays. Mention should also be made of Thomas Wode, a Reader at St Andrews, who was concerned that much fine music was being lost during the post-Reformation turbulence. To mitigate this, in collaboration with the composer David Peebles he compiled a collection of psalm settings and other pieces. This Wode Psalter includes no fewer than 106 psalms arranged in four-part harmony, lovingly collated in 'Partbooks' and beautifully illustrated with images of musicians, flowers, angels and birds. Thanks to a 2016 project involving Edinburgh's New College, the Church Service Society and St Mary's Church, Haddington, where Knox would have been baptised and later worshipped, these settings are again being learned, sung and recorded.

In a 1960 lecture given to the Presbyterian Historical Society of England, James Ross, then Minister of Paisley Abbey, outlined the form of Sunday worship in the autumn of 1560 in the fictional parish of Kilmarkie. The bell rings at 8 a.m. and people arrive, carrying stools on which to sit. The church is a plain rectangle with a pulpit half way down one side. The old altar and associated images have all been removed. Men sit on one side, women on the other. At 8.30 the Reader, who was formerly the parish priest, arrives. Like many former priests he has accepted the Reformed faith but is not judged sufficiently educated to preach. He reads from the English Prayer Book of 1552. It will be another two years before the revised Scottish *Book of Common Order* is published. As Kilmarkie has no tradition of innovating, it will probably be a few years after that before it appears there. Metrical psalms are sung but, again, a Scottish psalter has not yet been produced, so English settings are used. There is neither choir nor musical accompaniment. Around 10 o'clock the Minister arrives. He is an Augustinian canon at a local priory, well educated and familiar with Reformed doctrine, which he now embraces. He preaches a sermon that lasts about one hour. This is followed by an offering taken for the poor of the parish, collected in a box on the end of a long pole. Such 'ladles' are used to this day at Bowden Kirk in the Scottish Borders. Prayers and the benediction conclude the service at around 11.30 a.m. and the people disperse. After an interval of some two hours, people gather again for the catechising of children. This is followed by a service of Evening Prayer, led by the Reader from the Prayer Book. The day's worship concludes around 4 p.m. Communion is celebrated two or three times in the year, though some ministers would like to have the Sacrament more frequently. On a communion Sunday the first service would be at 5 a.m. for household servants, the second at 9 a.m. Communicants sit on benches at long tables, passing the bread and wine from hand to hand. The services again follow the order of the 1552 English Prayer Book. Kneeling for prayer is still practised by some but not for the receiving of the elements. These consist of unleavened shortbread and claret mixed with water and are brought in by the elders at the appropriate point in the service. Before breaking the bread the minister washes his hands in a bowl of water placed on the communion table for this purpose. The Sacrament would be received after fasting.

The Return and Departure of the Queen

The young King François II of France, husband of Mary Queen of Scots, had died in December 1560 at the age of sixteen. His ten-year-old brother succeeded as Charles IX and their mother, the powerful Catherine de Medici, assumed the Regency. In such circumstances there was no long-term future for a former Queen Consort. Of course Mary was also a queen in her own right, though thirteen years had passed since her mother sent her to France; and that mother was now also dead. Where else could she go but back to Scotland?

Such a move would certainly be welcomed by the Catholic hierarchy and, indeed, the Archbishop of Glasgow had been with Mary in France for some months. Also encouraged by the prospect was the Earl of Huntly, a prominent Catholic noble who was developing plans to raise an army to place Mary on the throne of a Scotland reclaimed for the Catholic Church. Protestant lobbyists were also bending her ear. Mary's half-brother, Lord James Stewart, offered to support her claim to the throne of England, if only to the extent of seeking to persuade Elizabeth to acknowledge Mary as her legitimate heir. No doubt such blandishments helped persuade Mary to return to Scotland as Queen. Nevertheless, she would have left the lively French court with a heavy heart and a real sense of bereavement. This being the case, the dreich and drizzly weather that greeted her arrival at Leith must perfectly have matched her mood, while for John Knox the elements were a clear sign of divine displeasure. Royal displeasure on the part of Queen Elizabeth was also registered. Mary's plan had been to travel through England but Elizabeth vetoed this, forcing her to make the longer sea journey. After all, Mary had still to put her name to the Treaty of Edinburgh and commit herself to a new and positive relationship with England.

Given Scotland's acceptance of the Reformation, Mary's strong commitment to Catholicism inevitably became a source of tension. On the Sunday after her arrival, Mass was said at Holyrood. This led to a mob threatening to invade the palace. In his sermon in St Giles' the following Sunday, Knox declared his view that 'one Mass was more fearful (to him) than ten thousand armed men'. He duly received a royal summons to explain himself, the first of four bruising encounters between him and Mary. From the queen's perspective she was content to recognise the Reformed Church and allow it to develop its policies. All she asked was that she be allowed to practise her own religion in the manner to which she had been accustomed since childhood. Today this sounds entirely reasonable. To Knox in 1561 it was the thin end of a very dangerous wedge which, given half a chance, would undermine all for which he and his fellow Reformers had striven and sacrificed.

It was not long before the question of Mary's marriage arose, and there was no shortage of potential suitors. Her eventual choice was her cousin Henry Stewart, Lord Darnley, and they were married at Holyrood on 29 July 1565. The ceremony included a Mass in which the bridegroom did not participate. Darnley had royal blood in his veins. His mother was a daughter of Margaret Tudor by her second husband, the Earl of Angus. His father was the Earl of Lennox and a descendant of a daughter of James II. Darnley thus had connections to both Scottish and English royal families. Such a lineage created tensions among courtiers, and Mary's half-brother, James Stewart, by then Earl of Moray, was particularly displeased. One famous casualty of the court jealousy and intrigue was an Italian musician, David Rizzio. He had become a favourite of the queen, serving also as her private secretary. In the gossipy atmosphere of the palace this gave rise to speculation as to just how close they were. The outcome was Rizzio's brutal murder in the presence of the heavily pregnant queen. Several courtiers were in her company at the time, as was Darnley.

In June 1566, three months after the murder of Rizzio, the queen gave birth to a son, who would become James VI of Scotland and James I of England. Court tensions continued, and the following February Darnley was killed at Kirk o'Field, not far from Holyrood. Almost from the beginning, relations between the queen and Darnley had been strained. Following the murder of Rizzio they had deteriorated even further. There were also whisperings of an affair between Mary and the Earl of Bothwell, who became chief suspect in Darnley's murder. Not surprisingly, these suspicions grew stronger when, three months after the murder, Bothwell and Mary married, he having been conveniently acquitted in a show trial. The marriage divided the country, and a month later forces loyal and opposed to Mary clashed at Carberry Hill. The outcome was defeat for the queen and her eventual imprisonment in Loch Leven Castle. There she miscarried twins, Bothwell's children. At this lowest point of vulnerability she was coerced into abdicating in favour of her young son, something she always maintained rendered the abdication illegal. A plot, of which she was the likely instigator, enabled her to escape from Loch Leven and to link up with a force of several thousand that had gathered in her cause of reclaiming the throne. The battle took place at Langside, to the south of Glasgow, on 13 May 1568. Mary's supporters faced a force led by her half-brother, the Earl of Moray, who won the day. Following this defeat Mary, with a small group of followers, fled south-west, eventually crossing the Solway and seeking sanctuary in England. This was not a wise move and nineteen years later she was executed on the orders of her royal cousin Elizabeth. She never saw Scotland or her son again. On 29 July 1567, just five days after his mother's forced abdication, James' coronation had taken place at the Kirk of the Holy Rude in Stirling, the third successive monarch to be crowned as an infant. John Knox preached the sermon and Moray, a committed Protestant, was appointed Regent.

Securing the Reformation

The outcome of these events was a firmer placing of Church and Crown in Protestant hands. Certainly things started well from that point of view, with the Regent calling a Parliament that put beyond challenge the legality of the 1560 proceedings. In particular, Parliament affirmed the *Confession of Faith* and required holders of office under the Crown and teachers in schools and universities to assent to it. Parliament also enacted three important pieces of legislation. These were:

- The Church Act, which gave legal establishment to the Church of Scotland as a Protestant body and declared it to be 'the only trew and haly Kirk of Jesus Christ within this realme'.
- The Church Jurisdiction Act, which declared 'thair is na uther face of Kirk nor uther face of Religion that is presentlie by the favour of God establisheit within the Realme'.
- The Coronation Oath Act, which required the monarch to protect the Reformed Church and root out all those opposed to its teaching.

In addition there were some positive adjustments to the Church's financial arrangements. Ministerial stipends were declared to be a first charge on the tax levied on the old Church benefices, leading to ministers being paid at least more regularly, if not more generously. Also on the positive side, Parliament declared that as benefices became vacant (many were still held by pre-Reformation clergy), the patron should identify a suitably qualified person to be examined by the Superintendent as to eligibility for the charge. By this means the numbers of Reformed ministers gradually increased.

Notwithstanding such moves the Reformation was far from secure. Scotland descended into a period of civil war between supporters of the banished queen, who sought Mary's restoration (the Queen's Men) and the King's Men, who thoroughly welcomed the new regime. A rival contender to Moray for the Regency, supported by his powerful Hamilton family, was the old Earl of Arran, who had previously held that office. Moray prevailed but three years later he was assassinated while passing through Linlithgow. The Earl of Lennox, Darnley's father, became Regent but the following year he was fatally injured in a brawl with supporters of the queen's party. Next was the Earl of Mar, who died within the year, to be succeeded in 1572 by the Earl of Morton. At last there was a period of some stability, with Morton, a determined supporter of a strong alliance with England, ruling on behalf of the young king.

It fell to Morton to resolve a major ecclesiastical crisis arising from the assassination of Moray. The deed had been carried out by a member of the Hamilton family, with the fatal shot fired from a house co-owned by Archbishop Hamilton of St Andrews. He was very much a queen's man, having baptised the infant James VI at Stirling Castle. He was also at Mary's side during the fateful Battle of Langside. For the King's Men these connections seemed too much of a coincidence. The archbishop was arrested and put on trial, not only for the assassination of Moray but also for the murder of Darnley five years previously. On 6 April 1571 he was hanged in Stirling. By these drastic means arose the first Episcopal vacancy since the Reformation.

The Regent Mar appointed John Douglas, Rector of St Andrews University, to replace Hamilton. Douglas had good credentials, having embraced the Reformed faith and contributed to both the *Confession of Faith* and *The First Book of Discipline*; but he was an old man, in poor health, quite unfit physically for the role. The suspicion was that his appointment was simply a device to keep the rich benefice in being and avoid any proper assessment of how the role was to be discharged under the new church system. The protests led to the calling of a General Assembly, which met at Leith in January 1572 and established a Commission to resolve the matter in consultation with the Privy Council. From this emerged the Concordat of Leith, which allowed the Crown to appoint bishops, subject to the Church's approval, thereby giving the Church the opportunity of ensuring that the financial resources attached to the bishopric were used for Church purposes. The trade-off was that new bishops, duly vetted and appointed, would take an oath of allegiance to the Crown though, ecclesiastically, they would be subject to the General Assembly. There was also a provision, enacted by Parliament in 1573, which required that all holders of ecclesiastical benefices should publicly subscribe the *Confession of Faith*. This, at any rate, was the theory. In practice the Regent Morton appointed his own men to bishoprics as they became vacant, by-passing potentially inconvenient church scrutiny of his nominees. Consequently, funds intended for diocesan purposes were diverted into the pockets of the Regent's political allies and the disparaging term 'tulchan' became attached to the bishops thus appointed. The term referred to straw-filled calf skins used by farmers to delude their cattle into believing they were the real thing and increase their supply of milk.

By this time another significant event had occurred in the story of the Scottish Reformation. John Knox died on 24 November 1572. He was aware of developments following the Leith General Assembly and as good as predicted that things would not work out entirely as hoped for with regard to directing church funds for exclusively church purposes. One of his last acts was to call for all bishops to give a full account of the financial stewardship of the diocese or archdiocese. He himself had declined the role of Superintendent having more than enough to do as Minister of St Giles'. In recording Knox's death it is appropriate to mention that he had been predeceased by his wife Marjorie, who had died towards the end of 1560, that decisive year for the Scottish Reformation. Not only had Marjorie been a loving wife and mother, she had given invaluable secretarial support to Knox, whose correspondence and writing were considerable. A little over three years later he had married Margaret Stewart, with whom he had three daughters.

Andrew Melville and *The Second Book of Discipline*

Andrew Melville was born near Montrose in 1545. The young Andrew was a bright boy, progressing from school to St Andrews University then to the University of Paris. He had a particular aptitude for languages and demonstrated proficiency in Latin, Greek, Hebrew and Syriac. In Paris he took an interest in educational method, something that he was to bring back to his native Scotland. He also studied law and eventually moved from Paris, via Poitiers to Geneva, where he was appointed a professor in the Academy. He was in Geneva at the time of the 1572 St Bartholomew's Day Massacre of French Protestants, which resulted in an influx of refugees seeking sanctuary in the city. Their experiences were to have a significant influence on him.

Two years later he returned to Scotland and was appointed Principal of Glasgow University. There he introduced fresh ideas from the continent, creating new courses and appointing professors to teach a range of subjects including science, philosophy, theology and languages. From Glasgow he moved to Aberdeen in 1575, where he introduced similar changes before being appointed Principal of St Mary's College, St Andrews, in 1580. He was also active in church affairs, serving as Moderator of the General Assembly in 1578. However, he was not prepared to take a 'softly, softly' approach on the unresolved issue of bishops and their role in the Reformed Church. His opposition rested on the grounds that Episcopacy effectively subordinated the Church to the State, since not only were bishops appointed by the Crown, but they also sat in Parliament.

In the years immediately following 1560 the art of the possible had led the Reformed Church to operate a 'mixed economy' in terms of its governance. As previously noted, some kirk sessions were already in place before 1560, having evolved from the privy kirks of the 1550s. These continued, with their numbers added to and elders co-operating with ministers at parish level. From December 1560 through to the 1580s, General Assemblies had been meeting annually; sometimes more than once a year. It was at the middle level of governance that things were less clear cut. *The First Book of Discipline* provided for ten districts each to be overseen by a Superintendent. Appointments were made to some of these positions, while three reform-inclined pre-Reformation bishops continued in their sees. At this stage the issue was not so much with the term 'bishop' as such; rather with the way the office had developed in the mediaeval Church. Bishops had become more and more engaged in civil affairs, holding high office in the land and siphoning off church revenues at the expense of the parishes and priests on the ground. Corruption had also entered through the right of the Crown to appoint bishops and, in a country far from Rome, there was little effective papal oversight. In the early years, therefore, the primary concern of the Reformers was with the character and performance of the post-holder. The term 'bishop' had certainly acquired a negative resonance, but the pastoral and leadership role the office was intended to provide was recognised as both good and necessary for the Church. Indeed, around this time a satirical distinction was made between three types of bishop: 'my Lord bishop' who was the grand prelate wielding both ecclesiastical and temporal power; 'my Lord's bishop', who owed his appointment to a powerful noble who, in return, benefited from the revenues of the diocese; and 'the Lord's bishop', who was the genuine man of God, caring for the clergy and people of his diocese.

Andrew Melville was not interested in such distinctions between 'good' and 'bad' bishops. His objection was to the office itself. For him all ministers were equal and answerable to the Church for the discharge of their duties; and for this purpose of accountability the Church should be represented, not by a higher-ranking individual, but by a superior court. Already ministers were meeting in local groups for prayer and Bible study in what became known as 'the Exercise'. It was but a step to develop these gatherings into a tier of local church government and to call them 'presbyteries' – gatherings of presbyters. Such presbyteries, overseeing the local Church, would be made up of ministers and elders. As for the regional level, in Melville's' view, there was no need to argue over the relative merits of Bishop versus Superintendent, for both offices were irrelevant. Let there be a court higher than the Presbytery but below the General Assembly and let this court be called the Synod. Finally, at the highest level, came the General Assembly, overseeing the whole work of the Church. Each court would be chaired by a rotating moderatorship on a 'first among equals' basis. This was the clear vision of Melville, set out in *The Second Book of Discipline* and aimed at providing an orderly shape to the Kirk that was emerging from the Reformation struggle.

Another issue for Melville was the distinction between Church and State, the Kingdom of God and the kingdom ruled over by an earthly Sovereign. Pre-Reformation Scotland had been governed by the king who, effectively, appointed the leading clergy, who then became courtiers and holders of government offices. The doctrine of Divine Right was held strongly by the Stewart kings and, for James, an essential aspect of this was a calling to rule over both Church and State. In a famous clash at Falkland Palace, Melville boldly informed his monarch that 'there are two kings and two kingdoms in Scotland. There is Christ Jesus the King and His kingdom is the Kirk, whose subject James the Sixth is, and of whose kingdom not a king, nor a lord, nor a head, but a member.' Perhaps this was still ringing in the royal ears when he observed in 1604, by which time he was also King of England, that Presbyterianism 'agreeth with monarchy as God and the devil'.

Meanwhile, back in late-1570s Scotland, opposition to Morton's Regency was growing and, in any event, the young James was reaching an age at which he might choose by whose influence to be guided and, indeed, to begin to rule in his own right. Technically his minority ended in 1578, though it would be another five years before he gained effective control of his country. In September 1579 Esmé Stewart, a cousin of Lord Darnley, James' late father, arrived from France and quickly became a favourite at court. His commission and not so hidden agenda was to persuade James back towards the old French/Catholic alliance. Stewart quickly found favour with the young king and it was not long before he was elevated to the earldom of Lennox. His rise continued apace and before long he was Duke of Lennox, the only dukedom in Scotland at the time. Inevitably, this created jealousies and rivalries at court. The French connection, too, was an unsettling factor, not least as Queen Mary was still alive and maintaining an effective communications network from her English prison at Fotheringay.

Adding to this political turbulence were rumours of a plan to overthrow the church reforms of the previous twenty years and restore the old ecclesiastical structure. The story was that the Pope had granted dispensations allowing Catholics in Scotland to subscribe and swear whatever might be required of them, provided they remained faithful to their religion and ready to advance its interests – Nicodemism in another guise! Whether true or not, such scaremongering served to strengthen Protestant feeling, leading in 1581 to the drafting and mass signing of a document that became known as the King's or Negative Confession. King James himself subscribed. In what today we would call 'colourful' language, this stressed the 'negatives' in the Roman Catholic religion and bound the signatories to accept 'the true religion', to defend the king, the Gospel and the nation. Ministers, on pain of a deduction from stipend, were exhorted 'to crave the same confessioun of their parochiners and instructed to proceed against refusers according to our lawes and order of the Kirk'.

In August 1582 there arose a dramatic turn of events in which the young king was seized by a group of staunchly

Protestant nobles. Known as the 'Ruthven Raid' from its leader, William Ruthven, Earl of Gowrie, the captors held the king for ten months, with Ruthven acting as head of an ultra-Protestant regime. Unsurprisingly, the raiders had the approval of the General Assembly, where Andrew Melville had considerable influence. However, any advantage was short lived and, indeed, the Assembly was to pay a price for its support of the raid. Once the king was free, power passed to James Stewart, recently ennobled as Earl of Arran and a close associate of Esmé Stewart. This new Arran was no friend of Melville and in 1584 Parliament, under his influence, passed a series of measures that, in Presbyterian lore, became known as the 'Black Acts'. These asserted the power of the king over the Church as well as the State. Any gathering of subjects for civil or ecclesiastical purposes would require royal permission, including General Assemblies; presbyteries were condemned and ministers were forbidden to criticise the king and his policies in their sermons. The power of bishops was also confirmed. Indeed, additional powers were given to the Archbishop of St Andrews and to the bishops to 'put order to all matters and causes ecclesiastical within their dioceses'. To illustrate these shifting sands betwixt Episcopal and Presbyterian polity it may be noted that the Archbishop of St Andrews, Patrick Adamson, had been Moderator of the General Assembly in 1576, the year of his consecration as archbishop.

It was not long before the tide turned again, and in 1585 the Synod of Fife excommunicated Adamson for his contribution to the passing of the 'Black Acts' and for setting himself above his fellow ministers. Encouraged by this, a number of ministers began to preach against royal policy. Fortunately for them, the king, now ruling in his own right, adopted a diplomatic approach that led to the drafting of Articles of Accommodation and the convening of a General Assembly in 1586. Catching the mood of conciliation, the Assembly rescinded the Synod's excommunication of Adamson and instructed those preachers who had criticised the king to apologise. It also adopted a pattern of presbyteries that more or less covered the country and accepted that the bishops should serve as moderators of the presbyteries within whose bounds they resided. However, such all-round goodwill could not last. Within the year a vacancy arose in the bishopric of Caithness and the king was minded to appoint Robert Pont, minister of St Cuthbert's, Edinburgh. The response of the General Assembly was to concur in the royal appreciation of Pont's qualities, but to point out that he was 'already a bishop according to the doctrine of St Paul ... but as to that corrupt estate or office of them who have been termed bishops heretofore, we find it not agreeable to the Word of God ... neither is the said Mr Robert willing to attempt the same in that matter.' The royal response was to annex the landed properties of bishoprics, abbeys and other prelacies to the Crown. The Church didn't want bishops; the king needed money and saw his opportunity. Eventually though, in 1592, Parliament passed legislation that established a fully-fledged Presbyterian regime of Kirk session, Presbytery, Synod and General Assembly. The right of the Assembly to meet annually, in the presence of the king or his Commissioner, was affirmed, as was the freedom of the Assembly to meet at other times, if required. Episcopal jurisdiction was abolished and ministerial appointments were declared to lie with presbyteries. This 1592 Act is sometimes referred to as the Great Charter of the Church, though, given the nature of royal and ecclesiastical politics of the time, it would not be long before it was challenged and undermined.

THE SEVENTEENTH CENTURY

Throughout the seventeenth century the Kirk had periods of Episcopalian and Presbyterian government. The Presbyterian polity affirmed in 1592 held until replaced in 1610 by an Episcopalian regime. That lasted until 1638, when the Presbyterians regained control. In 1661, Episcopalianism returned and held sway until 1690, when the Kirk finally became established as Presbyterian. Since then there have been separations and reunions but, essentially, that settlement has continued to the present.

From Burntisland via London to Aberdeen and Perth

We begin this century's story in the Fife coastal town of Burntisland, and we start with the Bible.

Burntisland was a significant seaport, second only to Leith. Such, indeed, was the town's importance that a new church, dedicated to St Columba, was built there in 1592 – the first following the Reformation. The General Assembly of 1601 had been appointed to meet in Edinburgh, in the presence of the king. However, due to an outbreak of plague the venue was changed to St Andrews. At the last minute it was altered again. James had injured his shoulder in a hunting accident while staying at Rossend Castle, so summoned the Assembly to meet in nearby Burntisland. A significant outcome of that Assembly was a decision to commission a new translation of the Bible. Two years later James succeeded to the English throne and moved south. There work on the project got underway and in 1611 the 'Authorised' or 'King James' version duly appeared. In passing it is interesting to note that the General Assembly of

1946 received an Overture from the Presbytery of Stirling and Dunblane in the same vein. This had been introduced by the Reverend G. S. Hendry, and it recommended 'that a translation of the Bible be made in the language of the present day'. The Assembly approved the proposal and resolved to approach other Churches with a view to taking it forward. The outcome was the New English Bible.

While Queen Elizabeth had always been reluctant to acknowledge her successor, there was no disputing the legitimacy of James' claim to the English throne. His mother, Mary Queen of Scots, and his father, Lord Darnley, were both direct descendants of Henry VII, and Elizabeth had no children. Undoubtedly James' succession was eased by a spirit of Protestant co-operation between Scotland and England post-1560. Reform-minded Scots had sought refuge south of the border during periods of Catholic resurgence, rubbing shoulders with their English counterparts in Church and State. In addition, James' low-key response to his mother's execution, while perhaps unnatural from a family point of view, was astute politically, not least in light of threats such as the Spanish Armada the following year. Elizabeth died on 24 March 1603. On Sunday 3 April, James worshipped with the congregation in St Giles' and a few days later set off for London. Given his Episcopal leanings he soon felt very much at home there and entered with relish into his role as Supreme Governor of the Church of England. At the same time he was determined to create a sense of unity – indeed uniformity – between his distinctive kingdoms, not least in matters ecclesiastical. His aim was one Protestant Church for England and Scotland, governed by bishops and using Episcopalian forms of worship.

Before leaving for London, James had maintained pressure on the Scots to appoint bishops. Using his power to determine the time and place of General Assemblies, he selected venues such as Perth, Dundee and Montrose, thus making it easier for ministers from beyond the central lowlands to attend. Not only did this widen the constituency; it set up a north–south tension. An Assembly at Dundee in 1597 had appointed a Commission with powers to negotiate with the king on church matters and from this emerged a desire for ecclesiastical representation in Parliament. This was taken forward by Parliament recommending that ministers holding the rank of bishop should exercise this role, and by 1600, despite opposition from subsequent Assemblies in Dundee and Montrose, James had appointed bishops to Caithness, Ross and Aberdeen, who duly took their seats in Parliament. Once settled in London, James continued to assert his authority over the Scottish Church. For example, he postponed an Assembly called for Aberdeen in 1604; however, ignoring the royal edict, a number of ministers still met. Summoned to explain themselves they declined to appear and were exiled. Two years later a Kirk delegation, which included Andrew Melville, was called to London for discussions on unifying the churches north and south of the border, on Episcopalian lines. For Melville this was a non-starter but others, such as John Spottiswoode, Archbishop of Glasgow, were more compliant. The outcome was that by 1610 the Scottish Church was again administered by bishops.

Building on this success, James pressed on with his plans for a common liturgy for Scotland and England. In 1616 a General Assembly met in Aberdeen, with the Earl of Montrose representing the king. From this emerged a new Confession of Faith, a catechism for schools and a new liturgy for church services. In connection with the last of these the king had ordained that a uniform liturgy for Divine Service be 'set down to be read in all kirks ... to the end the common people may be acquainted therewith, and by custom may learn to serve God rightly'. In particular the king proposed five new 'canons' or 'articles' setting out specific liturgical instructions. Sensing the explosive nature of what was proposed, the bishops demurred and relayed their concerns to the king.

The following year (1617) James made his only visit back

to Scotland and had the chapel at Holyrood furnished to accommodate Anglican rites. At the same time he sought to stiffen the resolve of the bishops, reminding them of his authority over matters spiritual as well as temporal. The outcome was a carefully selected Assembly to meet at Perth on 15 August 1618. As no election of a Moderator took place, Archbishop Spottiswoode presided on the basis that Perth was in his diocese. The 'Five Articles of Perth', as they became known, were duly presented. These provided for kneeling to receive Holy Communion, permission to administer the Sacrament in private to the sick, permission to baptise in private houses, Confirmation by the bishop of children at the age of eight years and the observance of Christmas, Good Friday, Easter, Ascension and Pentecost. Before a vote was taken, Spottiswoode informed the Assembly that votes would be recorded, with those disapproving having their names passed to the king and their stipends withheld. The Articles were duly approved by 86 in favour to 49 against. Scornful of the threats, nearly all the ministerial members had voted against. Throughout the country there was strong resistance and a number of non-compliant ministers were subject to legal proceedings. It has to be said, though, that on the whole the bishops were reluctant to force obedience, hoping that, in time, the new ways would be accepted peacefully.

From James to Charles to Jenny Geddes

King James VI and I died on 27 March 1625 at the age of fifty-eight. As in Scotland, so during his twenty-two years in England ecclesiastical politics had featured prominently throughout his reign. Just two years after the move south a Catholic plot to blow up king and Parliament was averted. The ringleader, Guido Fawkes, and his fellow conspirators were executed and to this day their 'gunpowder plot' is commemorated every 5 November. In a way this was helpful to James in that it led to a surge in anti-Catholic sentiment and strengthened his position as a Protestant monarch. However, Catholicism was not the only challenge to Anglicanism. Foreshadowing problems that would assail his successor. James also had to contend with a strong Puritan faction. This was no friend to bishops or the practices of the Church of England. Indeed, within twenty years of James' death there would develop what he would certainly have regarded as an 'unholy alliance', namely English Puritans and Scottish ultra-Presbyterians singing from the same psalm sheet.

In 1625 James was succeeded by his second son, Charles. The elder son, Prince Henry, a young man of great promise, had died of typhoid in 1612 at the age of eighteen. Charles was born at Dunfermline in 1600. When his parents left for London the three-year-old prince did not accompany them. A delicate child, he was left behind in the care of nurses, but after a year was considered well enough to make the journey south. The test was that he could walk the length of the great hall of Dunfermline Palace unaided. At the age of twenty-three he was dispatched to Madrid to pursue the prospect of a marriage to the Infanta Maria of Spain, but differences of religion created insuperable obstacles. The Infanta was not minded to become a Protestant, and for Charles to convert to Catholicism, a Spanish condition of the marriage, would have been politically unthinkable. However, all was not lost. On the way to Spain the young Charles had broken his journey at the French court in Paris. There he set eyes on the Princess Henrietta Maria, sister to the French king, and two months after his succession they married in Canterbury.

Like his father, Charles was strongly committed to the principle of Divine Right, which brought him into conflict with both the English Parliament and Church. When Parliament refused to support his policies he dissolved it and attempted to rule by royal decree. At the same time the Anglican Church was wary of the queen's adherence to her Catholic faith and concerned over her influence, and that of her chaplains, upon the king. Religious affairs were further complicated by the presence of Puritans, Congregationalists and Presbyterians. To the Anglican establishment these 'Independents' represented as much a threat as Catholicism.

Against this complex background Charles nevertheless persisted with his scheme to impose a common policy on the English and Scottish churches. The opportunity to assert his will arose when, in 1633, he came to Scotland to be crowned King of Scots. The ceremony took place on 18 June in the Chapel Royal at Holyrood which was, once again, fitted out for Anglican worship. In Charles' retinue was William Laud, Bishop of London, soon to become Archbishop of Canterbury. Laud was given the role of master of ceremonies, a move hardly designed to win friends within the Scottish Church and Parliament. On the Sunday after the coronation the king worshipped at St Giles'. The service had barely begun with the accustomed Bible readings when the Reader was ordered to stand aside as two of Laud's chaplains, dressed in Anglican surplices, took over. From that point onwards worship was conducted according to the English Book of Common Prayer. The outrage created by such disrespect to Scottish custom is not difficult to imagine.

At this time the interior of St Giles' was divided by an internal wall into an East Kirk and a Great Kirk, home to two congregations. To the king this was quite unacceptable and he instructed that the whole space be opened up so that St Giles' could be used as one great cathedral. Moreover, Charles had further decreed that the historic Archdiocese of St Andrews be divided, with the territory lying to the south of the Forth raised to a new Diocese of Edinburgh. The new diocese, of course, would require its own bishop and, by the same logic, the new bishop would require his cathedral. So, on 29 September 1633, Charles issued a royal charter erecting a bishopric and declaring St Giles' to be the Cathedral for the City and Diocese of Edinburgh. It is also relevant to note that similar instructions were issued with regard to the repair of other great churches, including the cathedrals in Glasgow, Dornoch, Dunkeld, Iona and St Andrews.

The policy was clear: the Scottish Kirk would follow the pattern of the Church of England. Having ruled as to the style and layout of church buildings, Charles turned his attention to the question of liturgy. The Scottish bishops had not pushed the Five Articles of Perth and worship had largely continued along the lines of Knox's *Book of Common Order*. Once again Charles took control. The bishops were instructed to prepare a Code of Canons that would address matters of church government and liturgy. In addition, they would suffer the indignity of having Archbishop Laud correct their homework. Unsurprisingly, the resultant liturgy was modelled on the English Prayer Book,

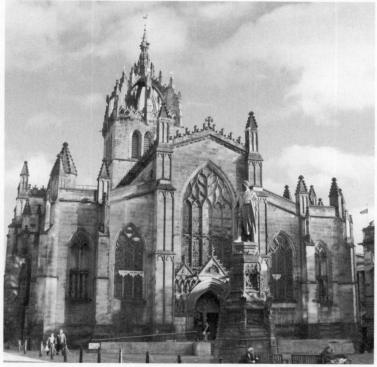

St Giles' Cathedral.

subject to token gestures such as substituting 'presbyter' for 'priest'. The Scottish practice of sharing communion round a table was swept away with new instructions for a Holy Table at the east end of the church. In front of this the minister would consecrate the bread and wine, standing with his back to the congregation. This flew completely in the face of the Reformed view of the Sacrament as a shared meal presided over by a minister, as distinct from a purported sacrificial offering by a mediating priest.

The new Prayer Book, which became known as 'Laud's Liturgy', was published in the spring of 1637, though its introduction was delayed until July of that year. This was in order to allow time for people to become familiar with it. What happened when it was first used in St Giles' on Sunday 23 July is the stuff of legend. The church was full, with many dignitaries present, including Archbishop Spottiswoode of St Andrews (by then also Chancellor of Scotland), the Bishop of Edinburgh, members of the Privy Council and the Town Council. No sooner had Dean Hannay begun to read from the new Prayer Book than a riot ensued. People shouted their disapproval of 'popery'; missiles were hurled, including the stools people would bring to sit on. The name Jenny Geddes, traditionally thrower of the first stool, has come down in history along with her reported outburst: 'Dinna say Mass at my lug' (Don't say Mass in my ear). Eventually the protesters were removed, but they continued to barrack outside as the service continued, jostling the archbishop as he departed. Acknowledging the strength of feeling, and also betraying its own doubts as to the wisdom of the policy being pursued, the Privy Council, headed by Archbishop Spottiswoode, took the decision to suspend the Prayer Book pending further advice from the king. As might have been expected, the king's advice was that his royal will should be obeyed.

With Charles back in London and those in authority in Scotland aware of the feeling on the ground, this was not going to happen. Influential people began to organise and a great number of petitions were sent in from ministers, nobles and ordinary citizens, urging the continuation of worship in the form that had become accepted following the Reformation. In October 1637 there was a further and more substantial riot in Edinburgh, which was eventually quelled by an offer from the Privy Council to consult with representatives of the protesters. Towards the end of the year a deputation was sent to London to inform the king of the strength of feeling, but all this achieved was a reassertion of his determination that the Prayer Book should be used.

From the National Covenant to the Bishops' Wars

Faced with this impasse the response of the opposition was to set out their grievances in a document that became known as the National Covenant. This was drafted by Alexander Henderson, Minister at Leuchars parish church and Professor of Rhetoric and Philosophy at St Andrews University. The co-author was Archibald Johnston of Warriston, a young Edinburgh lawyer. The document was in three sections. It began with the text of the Negative Confession of 1581. This, it will be recalled, enumerated what the signatories considered to be errors in the teaching and practices of the mediaeval Church. Not only was the Confession itself reproduced; there was also a reminder that it had been signed by King James himself. There followed a list of Acts of Parliament in support of the Reformed Church. Presumably this legislative inventory was the work of Archibald Johnston. The third section included a commitment to resist the changes being forced upon the Church 'to the ruin of the True Reformed Religion and of our Liberties, Laws and Estates'. Along with this statement of intent was an affirmation of loyalty: 'We promise and swear that we shall to the utmost of our power stand to the defence of our dread Sovereign, the King's Majesty, his Person and Authority.' The term 'covenant' was drawn from the Bible, where it is used to describe the relation between God

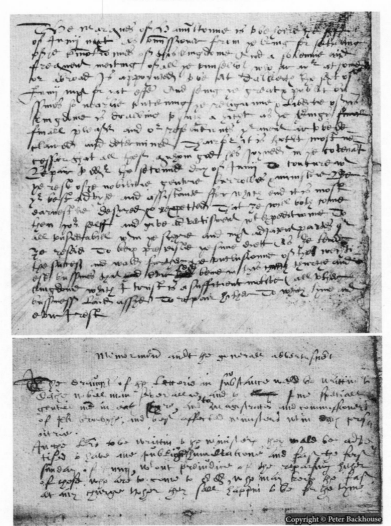

The National Covenant.

and the people. As such the Covenant expressed a potent mix of religion and politics and had the desired effect of uniting the people in powerful opposition to the king's policies.

On 26 February 1638 the Covenant was signed by members of the nobility in Edinburgh's Greyfriars Churchyard. Among the first to sign were two of Scotland's leading nobles, the Earl of Montrose and the Earl of Argyll. The following day opportunity to subscribe was given to ministers and the general public, and this was taken by many, with great enthusiasm. Thereafter copies were taken around the country, where townspeople and villagers added their signatures. Not all were swept up in the tide of protest and emotion. An exception was the episcopally inclined city of Aberdeen and its environs; also the Highlands remained largely detached. There are also indications that not all who signed did so willingly. Nevertheless, such an upsurge of public opinion was a clear challenge to the royal authority, notwithstanding the protestations of loyalty also expressed in the document. After some initial hesitation Charles responded by dispatching the Marquis of Hamilton, a London-based courtier, as his High Commissioner to Scotland. Hamilton was on record as having described the Covenanters as 'possessed by the devil', which hardly indicated objectivity. In any event he was no match for the supporters of the Covenant. Twice he had to return to London for fresh instructions, but eventually, in July, an offer was made: a General Assembly and a Parliament could be called and, while Episcopacy would be preserved, bishops would be answerable to the General Assembly. This reflected some movement, but a question remained as to the mode of appointment to General Assemblies. Charles favoured only clerical representation, while many of the Covenanters demanded the election of elders by presbyteries. Hamilton was summoned back to London for further instructions, returning in September with a further offer to revoke the Prayer Book and the Code of Canons.

A General Assembly duly met in Glasgow Cathedral on 21 November 1638, the first in twenty years. It was overseen by Hamilton as Lord High Commissioner, with Alexander Henderson as Moderator and Johnston of Warriston as Clerk. The following year Henderson would become Minister of St Giles'. The membership comprised 140 ministers and 98

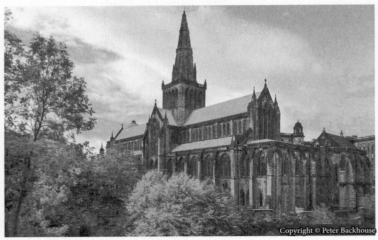

Copyright © Peter Backhouse

Glasgow Cathedral.

elders, including nobles, knights, landed proprietors and burgesses. The nobles included the Earls of Montrose, Lothian, Cassillis and Home. Members of the Privy Council were also in attendance, including the powerful Earl of Argyll who, along with Montrose, would feature notably in subsequent events, albeit on different sides. An observer commented that 'none had gowns, but many had doublets, swords and daggers'. The same observer went on to opine that 'if men had behaved in his house as rudely as they did in the house of God, he would have turned them downstairs'. After a week the Marquis of Hamilton dissolved the Assembly. In part this may have been driven by the bad behaviour. More probably it was in response to the policies being pursued, particularly a decision to abolish bishops. Giving greater weight to the authority of the Moderator than to that of the Commissioner, the Assembly declined to be dissolved, despite being threatened with a charge of treason. Over the coming weeks not only did it abolish Episcopacy; the bishops themselves were deposed and excommunicated. Other decisions declared the 'pretended' Assemblies between 1606 and 1618 to be 'unlawful and null'; likewise the Prayer Book and Canons and the Five Articles of Perth. The Assembly further determined that it was not appropriate for Church ministers to hold civil office by sitting in Parliament or acting as justices or judges in a civil court. This was a significant step firmly in line with Andrew Melville's doctrine of the two kingdoms. Finally, the right of the Church to call General Assemblies was affirmed, with the next Assembly proclaimed to be held in Edinburgh on the third Wednesday of July 1639, 'unless His Majesty should otherwise appoint' – an interesting diplomatic rider.

What followed, however, was not diplomacy but war between the king and his subjects. Even as he shuttled Hamilton back and forth, Charles was considering a military option for dealing with the Covenanters. In the summer of 1639 he led an English force to Berwick while a Scottish army encamped a few miles away, north of the border. An intriguing tale has come down that Hamilton's mother supported the Covenanters and had threatened to shoot her son should he ever set foot in Scotland as the head of an army. Meantime, various minor skirmishes took place between Scottish Royalist and Covenanting forces in Aberdeenshire. Further south the cross-border stand-off continued with neither side wanting a serious engagement, and in June 1639 a settlement known as the Pacification of Berwick was agreed. This provided for the disbanding of the Covenanting army in exchange for a commitment by the king to appoint a General Assembly to meet in August. The agreement also provided for a meeting of the Scottish Parliament following on from the General Assembly – all with a view to resolving the matters under dispute. For the king this was a triumph of hope over experience. The Assembly proceeded to confirm all the decisions taken the previous year in Glasgow, at which point Charles took steps to delay the promised meeting of Parliament. Meanwhile, he summoned an English Parliament with a view to raising funds to support a second Bishops' War against the Scots. In this he was unsuccessful and, within a month, dissolved what became known as the 'Short Parliament'. Frustrated by the royal delaying tactics, the Scottish Parliament convened in June 1640, in defiance of the king, and proceeded to ratify all the Acts of the General Assembly, including the abolition of bishops.

Maintaining the initiative, a covenanting force crossed the Tweed in August and, meeting no resistance, was able to occupy Northumberland and County Durham, including the city of Newcastle. Indeed, the English force was in retreat. In October Charles was forced to agree terms in the Treaty of Ripon, allowing the Scots to hold the territory gained against a pledge to meet their expenses. To honour this pledge Charles had no option but to summon another Parliament (the 'Long Parliament', as it came to be known), but there he found little sympathy or support. On the contrary, members attacked his government and impeached two of his principal supporters – the Earl of Stafford, his chief adviser, who had responsibility for resourcing the military campaign, and Archbishop Laud. Eventually, in August 1641 the English Parliament approved a payment of £300,000 to the Scots under the terms of the Treaty of Ripon and required Charles to give his assent to the Acts of the Scottish Parliament, including the one abolishing bishops.

Thus spurned by the English Parliament, Charles regrouped and headed north. He spent three months in Edinburgh, bestowing honours and attending services in St Giles' which, presumably, were not entirely to his taste. Down south the English Civil War was brewing and Charles needed every ally he could get. In an ironic way the tables were being completely turned. Charles had sought to unify Scotland and England through an ecclesiastical polity based on bishops and the Prayer Book. Now the Scottish Covenanters saw their opportunity and allied themselves with the English Nonconformists and Puritans. By this means they sought a unifying ecclesiastical polity based on Presbyterianism north and south of the border.

This new-found amity between Scottish Covenanters and English parliamentarians was clearly a friendship of convenience. Fearing the prospect of the king receiving support from Irish Catholic troops, the English parliamentarians welcomed the prospect of Scottish support. For their part the Covenanters were heartened by the prospect of Presbyterianism taking hold in England. This was certainly seen by the king's English opponents as a lesser evil than a return to Catholicism and there were, indeed, a significant number of Presbyterians within the English Parliament. In 1643 there emerged from these alliances a document known as 'The Solemn League and Covenant'. This was in effect a treaty with a threefold purpose: the preservation of the reformed religion in Scotland; the reformation of religion in England and Ireland 'according to the Word of God and the example of the best Reformed Churches'; and the 'extirpation of Popery and Prelacy'. A copy was signed in the East Kirk of St Giles' as well as at Westminster. Not all members of the English Parliament approved, with some switching to the Royalist side; but it was enough to persuade the Scots to send a covenanting army south to join forces with the English parliamentary army. However, not all Scots were comfortable taking up arms against the king. In particular James Graham, by now Marquis of Montrose, had become increasingly concerned at the turn of events and decided to place his considerable military acumen at the service of the king. To his dying day he professed his support for the Covenant to the extent that it resisted the power of the king over the Church; but to take up arms against the lawful Sovereign was, for him, a step too far.

In addition to these moves the English Parliament resolved to appoint an Assembly drawn from its own membership with a remit to consult on how the Church of England might be further reformed in order to make it 'most agreeable to God's holy Word … and nearer agreement with the Church of Scotland and other Reformed Churches abroad'. Clearly, there was a strong feeling within the Long Parliament that the Anglican settlement, with its Episcopal structure and the continuation of practices such as kneeling to receive the Sacrament, had not gone far enough to distinguish itself from the pre-Reformation Church. Naturally, the king did not approve of this development, and accordingly, those parliamentarians who were content with the way the Church of England functioned declined to serve. The Westminster Assembly, as it came to be known, first met in July 1643 and it was not long before an invitation was extended to the Church of Scotland to send representatives. Alexander Henderson, Moderator of the 1638 Assembly, was duly dispatched south along with Samuel Rutherford, a future Principal of St Mary's College, St Andrews, and others. Over the next few years the Assembly produced various documents, including a Directory for the Public Worship of God, the Westminster Confession of Faith, a Shorter and Longer Catechism and a Form of Church Government. This last document proved particularly controversial for, while all were opposed to Episcopacy, there were also those who were opposed to any arrangement that involved a layer of authority over individual congregations. For them Presbyterianism was every bit as objectionable as Episcopacy, and the only appropriate system was what we today call Congregationalism.

Of the various outcomes of the Westminster Assembly the one that was to have most enduring significance upon the Kirk was the Confession of Faith. This was adopted by the General Assembly of 1647, with some qualifications as to the power of the civil magistrate, and to this day remains the Church of Scotland's 'principal subordinate standard'. Effectively, the Westminster Confession superseded the 1560 *Scots Confession*. That document had been drawn up in the heat of the Reformation struggle and under pressure from Parliament. By contrast, the Westminster Confession was worked on by a large Assembly of churchmen and parliamentarians over many months, and the ensuing document was not only much longer but also more detailed in setting out a system of Christian belief, including the doctrine of predestination.

Predestination

The doctrine of predestination derives from St Augustine in the fifth century, though its origins go back before that. In Romans chapter 8 Paul tells his readers that 'all things work together for good for those who love God, who are called according to his purpose'. He continues: 'For those whom he foreknew he also predestined to be conformed to the image of his Son, in order that he might be the firstborn within a large family.'

Reference has been made to Luther's condemnation of indulgences. We saw how he took his stand on Scripture and that a defining moment came as he studied Paul's letter to the Romans. There, in chapter 1, verses 16 and 17, it is written: 'For I am not ashamed of the gospel; it is the power of God for salvation to everyone who has faith, to the Jew first and also to the Greek. For in it the righteousness of God is revealed through faith for faith: as it is written, "The one who is righteous will live by faith."' As he reflected on this, Luther became convinced that faith in and acceptance of Christ was the key to salvation. Good works were important, but they flowed from faith and were performed out of love of God and neighbour. The Christian needed no other motive and, certainly, not a motive of earning points towards salvation.

So far, so straightforward; but a question arises, namely, 'from where does faith come?' If it originates in our own decision to believe, might not that decision itself be characterised as a good work? That would immediately take us back to the position that salvation depends on deeds rather than faith. A possible solution would be to say that faith is itself a gift from God; but that then leaves us wondering why some receive the gift while others do not. A possible answer takes us back to predestination with its related concept of election. Faith being a gift of God, it is for God to choose on whom it is bestowed. Faith is thus a sign of divine election and explains why some have faith while others do not. Understood in this way the doctrine of predestination was a source of pastoral assurance in uncertain times, particularly to those who had sought refuge in Calvin's Geneva from persecution in other parts of Europe.

It is easy to caricature predestination. We might ask: If only faith counts, what is the point of being good rather than wicked; and how is it determined that some are heaven-bound while others are not? One answer was to assert that this was entirely a matter of divine predetermination; but this simply raised a whole raft of further questions. Did it mean, for example, that if you were one of the 'elect' then you could live out your years in wickedness and still make it to heaven? By contrast, if you were one of the 'damned', then no matter how saintly your life, it made not one whit of difference to your fate in the life to come. The poet Robert Burns captures the dilemma in his satirical poem 'Holy Willie's Prayer':

> O Thou, that in the heavens does dwell,
> Wha, as it pleases best Thysel',
> Sends aen to Heaven an' ten to Hell,
> A' for Thy glory,
> And no for onie gude or ill
> They've done afore Thee!

The whole poem goes on to record Holy Willie's sanctimonious self-righteousness. Despite his misdeeds he can still gloat over others who, as he sees it, lack his guarantee of salvation.

To the modern mind predestination makes little, if any, sense. It presumes an entirely arbitrary God and seems an extreme 'solution' to the issue raised by Luther's outrage at indulgences. Indeed, as a theory it feels just as repellent as the notion that people can buy their way into heaven. What about free will and personal responsibility? We teach children to choose the good rather than the evil. We also encourage them to accept responsibility for their mistakes and not to pass the blame to others. Why should the heavenly Father act differently with regard to his children? Surely the good we do must count somewhere in the equation; likewise the evil. The Calvinist response to such a challenge would be to argue that predestination in fact helps make sense of our freedom since God's election works through humans wills in such a way that, given the choice, the believer will choose the good over the evil.

Over the centuries the arguments for and against predestination ranged back and forth. In the early Church Augustine's chief opponent was a Celtic monk named Pelagius. He was appalled by the low moral standards he witnessed among some Christians and blamed these shortcomings on the doctrine. He argued that among the gifts God had given to humans was the capacity to discern between right and wrong and choose accordingly. This seems so sensible a theory that it is hard to believe that Pelagianism was once considered a most dangerous heresy. The objection to it was based on an extrapolation that argued that, ultimately, a human being might, by always choosing the right path, achieve salvation entirely on personal merit, with no need of a Saviour. In the Reformation period John Calvin espoused and developed the views of Augustine, and so the doctrine found its way into those churches that evolved from Calvin's teaching. That included the Church of Scotland through the influence of John Knox.

Not all who embraced the Reformation espoused predestination. In particular a Dutch theologian, Jakob Arminius, played Pelagius to Calvin's Augustine. He avoided the trap into which Pelagius fell when he seemed to hold open the prospect of human beings earning their own salvation. Arminius argued that, while Christ died to save everyone, God gave human beings the choice of believing or not believing in him. Accordingly, there was nothing inevitable about the decision the individual would make. Indeed, there are several instances in the Gospels where individuals decline the invitation to follow Jesus. Grace was freely offered to all, but not everyone embraced it. On this theory none could actually earn salvation through their own righteousness, for the first step towards salvation is always by the grace of God. However, the crucial choice of whether or not to take the step of acceptance lies with the human will.

Expressed like this we can understand why this teaching was to influence Methodist and Baptist theology. In the 1950s the American evangelist Billy Graham came to Scotland with his Tell Scotland Crusade, and over several weeks many rallies were held, attended by thousands. The climax of such events was the invitation to come forward and accept Christ. Many did and many did not, though who can say how lives were changed over ensuing years; but such events can perhaps illustrate Arminius' crucial point of grace being freely offered, and the individual having to make a choice. For the sixteenth- and seventeenth-century Reformers, though, his teaching was viewed as heretical. The Westminster Confession was uncompromising in its belief in predestination and this was to become one of the factors lying behind future divisions within the Kirk.

Civil War

The Westminster Assembly sat from 1643 to 1653. By the time it concluded its deliberations, much had changed in the wider political landscape, and the effects of the English civil war were being keenly felt in Scotland.

The Marquis of Montrose had been among the first to sign the National Covenant. He had also been active in the 1638 General Assembly and supportive of its decisions. However, he was less enamoured of the Solemn League and Covenant and could not find it in himself to take up arms against the king. More than that, he stood ready, willing and very able to take up arms against the king's enemies. Aware of this, Charles appointed Montrose his Viceroy in Scotland, and the army he raised, comprising largely fighters from Ireland and the Scottish Highlands, gained a series of spectacular victories against the forces of the Covenant. However, this run of successes came to an end in September 1645 with defeat at Philiphaugh, near Selkirk. Following this Montrose was forced to flee abroad.

Three months earlier, at the Battle of Naseby, Charles' supporters in England had suffered a major defeat at the hands of Oliver Cromwell's New Model Army. The king's response was to engage in yet another round of politicking and promising. He undertook to confirm the Solemn League and Covenant and to establish Presbyterian church government, albeit for a trial period of three years. If his plan had been to gain unequivocal Scottish support, it didn't work, for opinion north of the border was deeply divided. Some were prepared to give the king the benefit of doubt. They became known as 'Engagers', as they were prepared to enter into an 'Engagement' with Charles. Others, led by the Earl of Argyll, were strongly opposed to any dealings with him. They simply did not trust him, not least on the grounds of his consistent refusal to sign the Covenant. In the event the Engagers prevailed but, significantly, the most able Scottish generals supported Argyll and the non-Engagers and refused to lead any Scottish force sent to support the king. Nevertheless, an army was sent south under the command of the Duke of Hamilton. Battle was joined on 16 August 1648 at Preston, and the outcome was a devastating defeat for the Scots and Royalists. The scale of the loss can be gauged by the estimate of two thousand killed and nine thousand taken prisoner, compared with less than a hundred of Cromwell's army killed. Back in Scotland this left power in the hands of Argyll, who immediately began a purge of those of more moderate persuasion who had lent the king their support.

Meanwhile, events down south were moving apace, and on 31 January 1649 Charles was executed at Whitehall. Scotland immediately proclaimed his son Charles II, King of Scots. He was at Breda in Holland and a Scottish delegation was sent to treat with him there. Their mission was to offer him the throne of Scotland, but also to make clear that the offer was conditional upon his acceptance of the Covenants. Charles decided to play for time and assess what options of support might be open to him. Naturally, his thoughts turned to his late father's Viceroy,

Montrose, who was in exile in Norway. He accepted Charles' invitation to be his Lord Lieutenant in Scotland and made the sea crossing to Orkney. There he took command of a small fighting force and proceeded to make his way south, confident of gathering volunteers from disaffected clansmen on the way. However, these expectations were disappointed and an engagement at Carbisdale in Ross-shire with a force dispatched by Argyll ended in defeat. Montrose himself escaped capture, but only for a time. Those with whom he sought sanctuary betrayed him. He was arrested and taken to Edinburgh, where there could be only one outcome. His belief that he could be both Covenanter and Royalist was too subtle for his enemies. On 20 May 1650, Parliament sentenced him to death and the following day he was hanged. Thereafter, in the brutal manner of the time, his head was put on a spike at the Tolbooth, where it remained for ten years. His body was dismembered, with his limbs displayed in Stirling, Glasgow, Perth and Aberdeen

Following the execution of his Lord Lieutenant, Charles, still in Holland, entered into a treaty with the Scottish Parliament. This paved the way for his accession, though the price was still a commitment to support the Covenants with their aim of establishing Presbyterian church government in both Scotland and England. On this basis he arrived in Scotland on 23 June 1650, though the move did not play well with Cromwell. From his perspective this was a hostile act towards his English Commonwealth and he responded by invading Scotland. This led to the Battle of Dunbar, where the Scots army suffered a heavy defeat. The continuing tensions between extreme and moderate upholders of the Covenants inevitably had an undermining effect and no doubt contributed to the defeat by a much smaller English force. Indeed, Charles II himself soon became disillusioned with the fractious Covenanters; though he was savvy enough to recognise his need of their continuing support. He managed to do enough to retain that, and on 1 January 1651 he was crowned at Scone Abbey. The crown was placed on the royal head by the Earl of Argyll. Meanwhile, Cromwell remained a threat and, on the basis that attack was the best form of defence, Charles decided to take the battle to the enemy and invade England. Argyll and other prominent Covenanters again declined to take part and the venture ended in defeat at Worcester. It was after this setback that Charles famously sought refuge in a 'royal' oak tree at Boscobel House. Eventually he secured a more permanent refuge in France, which left Cromwell as Lord Protector, not only of England, but also of Scotland, Ireland and Wales. Almost a decade would pass before Charles ruled the entirety of his kingdom. Not until 23 April 1661 was his coronation at Scone complemented by an equivalent ceremony in Westminster Abbey. Once thus fully enthroned, Charles II, in line with the doctrine of Divine Right, asserted his

Copyright © Peter Backhouse

Montrose memorial.

position as head of both State and Church. As he saw it, just as the Sovereign delegated civil government to ministers of State, so Church government would be entrusted to bishops. As these bishops would owe their offices and benefits to the king, this would make them more pliable than the unpredictable alternative of presbyteries and General Assemblies. Things

Copyright © Peter Backhouse

Argyll memorial.

therefore looked bleak for the Covenanters, and one of the
first to pay the price was Argyll. The king, on whose head he
had placed the Scottish crown, had him arrested and charged
with high treason. A month after Charles' London coronation,
Argyll was executed and, in a spirit of nemesis, his head placed
on the Tolbooth spike, which for the previous decade had
displayed that of his adversary Montrose. More than that: only
a few days before Argyll's execution Montrose's remains were
gathered from around the country and he was given a belated
state funeral in St Giles'. The timing was clearly intended to
underscore the reversal of reputations. The lives of both men are
commemorated in nineteenth-century memorials at St Giles',
Argyll on the north side of the nave, Montrose on the south. On
Montrose's memorial are inscribed lines that he composed on
learning that he was to die:

> Scatter my ashes, Strew them in the air
> Lord, since thou knowest where all atoms are
> I'm hopeful Thou'lt recover once my dust
> And confident Thou'lt raise me with the Just.

Argyll's memorial bears the inscription: 'I set the crown on the
king's head. He hastens me to a better Crown than his own.'

The Return of the Bishop

In 1649, a week before the execution of Charles I, the Scottish Parliament had passed an Act of Classes that excluded from public office Royalists and those who had supported the Engagement with Charles. Argyll had been one of its leading proponents. In 1651 the Act was rescinded, a decision that created a serious division within the Scottish clergy between Resolutioners and Protesters. The former supported the resolution to repeal; the Protesters were vehement in their opposition. Essentially, the Resolutioners recognised the need to heal former divisions with a view to adopting a united approach to the nation's problems. By contrast, the Protesters maintained that these problems would be solved only when the people turned to God and honoured the Covenants.

Early in 1660 the Resolutioners dispatched James Sharp, minister at Crail, to London, with a brief to develop contacts helpful to the interests of Scottish Presbyterianism. The Resolutioner hope was that even if, as seemed probable, Episcopacy were to be fully re-established in England, the Scottish church might remain Presbyterian. In August 1660 Sharp returned to Edinburgh with a letter from the king that seemed to promise precisely this. However, it was not to be. When the Scottish Parliament met the following year it proceeded to enact a raft of policies that asserted the rights of the Crown and attributed all the recent troubles to a failure to respect the royal prerogative. Furthermore, Parliament went on to acknowledge the king as supreme governor of this kingdom over all persons and in all causes, to repudiate the Solemn League and Covenant and to declare that all assemblies held without royal assent were unlawful. Most concerning was an all-embracing Act of March 1661 that rescinded the legislation of 'pretended Parliaments' of the 1640s, including measures that had provided the legal underpinning of Presbyterian church government. Understandably, this set alarm bells ringing, though the volume at which these rang was far from uniform across the country. Acquiescence in the more Episcopally inclined north-east was counterbalanced by outrage in the Covenanting hotbed of the south-west. Unconcerned by protests (or less than fully briefed by his advisers), Charles proceeded to appoint bishops to all the Scottish sees. As only one of those nominated had been consecrated before the General Assembly of 1638, insult was added to injury when the other eight had to be consecrated in England. They all came from the Resolutioner wing of the Kirk, including the aforementioned James Sharp. He became Archbishop of St Andrews and Primate of Scotland.

The first task of the new bishops was to meet with their clergy, and synods were called for this purpose. Again the north-east/ south-west divide was apparent, the former being well attended while the latter were largely boycotted. Presbyteries remained as gatherings of ministers, though with no ecclesiastical authority, and kirk sessions continued to administer discipline at parish level. Eventually, though, a ticking time bomb exploded. In 1649 the Scottish Parliament had abolished patronage (the mechanism whereby local land owners presented new ministers to vacant parishes) but this legislation was among the statutes rescinded in 1661. Following this and adding insult to injury, a new Act of 1662 declared that all ministers inducted since the passing of the 1649 Act should now apply to the patron and bishop to have their appointments ratified. Again, in the north and east of the country many viewed this as a box-ticking exercise and were confirmed in their charges. However, in areas such as Ayrshire, Lanarkshire, Dumfries and Galloway, very few sought such regularisation of their appointments.

Faced with this defiance the Privy Council ruled that all who failed to comply by a given date would be deemed to have resigned their charges. When it became clear that the great majority was not prepared to be intimidated, a three-month extension was allowed. When that date came and went, with no change of mind, 270 ministers were removed from their churches and manses and their places filled by licentiates (trainee ministers) from other areas. Many of these came from Aberdeenshire, where Episcopalianism was strong; so much so that it was joked that farmers there could not find lads to herd their cattle as all had gone south to be 'curates'. This was the term used contemptuously to refer to the ill-qualified substitutes. The expelled ministers were ordered to remove themselves by a distance of at least twenty miles from their former charges, and members of their congregations were threatened with fines if they failed to attend the services conducted by the 'curates'. Again the great majority refused to bow to such threats, preferring to travel to open-air conventicles led by those they still regarded as their ministers.

These conventicles were soon declared illegal and troops were dispatched to break them up and impose fines upon those attending. Such action inevitably brought reaction in kind. In November 1666 Sir James Turner, commander of a posse of government troops deployed to enforce the law, was captured at Dumfries. The background to this venture lay in an incident at Dalry, where an elderly man by the name of John Grier, who was unable to pay a fine for not attending church, was beaten severely by some of Turner's soldiers. A group of four local Covenanters happened to be in the village. They went to Grier's rescue and pleaded with the soldiers to let the old man go. Swords were drawn and a pistol shot wounded one of the soldiers. The Covenanters were supported by villagers, who joined in the melee and disarmed the soldiers. By this stage a crowd of some ninety people had gathered. Realising that they would receive little mercy from Turner, they decided to take the battle to him and march on Dumfries where he was based. By the time they reached the town their number had grown to about 250 and there they captured Sir James, still in his night attire. Having come thus far they kept going, gathering numbers as they progressed. At Bridge of Doon they were joined by an experienced soldier who volunteered to take command of this little army, now expanded fourfold to some 900 men. Within days they were to face the full wrath of a government force sent to engage them before they reached the capital, for that is where they were heading to present a petition to Parliament. The unequal forces met on the slopes of the Pentland Hills near Colinton on the outskirts of Edinburgh. The engagement on 18 November 1666, known as the Battle of Rullion Green, ended disastrously for the Covenanters, who were given no quarter. An account of the aftermath tells of Sharp condemning to death eleven prisoners who had surrendered after being promised mercy. 'You were pardoned as soldiers', he is said to have explained, 'but you are not acquitted as subjects.'

A very different churchman from Sharp was Bishop Leighton of Dunblane, who urged mediated rather than military solutions to the increasingly bitter conflict between the Episcopalian and Presbyterian parties. One of his proposals was that the bishop's role should simply be that of permanent presbytery moderator, with no attendant hierarchical requirements such as ministers pledging canonical obedience to the bishop. In this same spirit of seeking compromise a government initiative of 1669 offered a royal indulgence that would enable 'outed' ministers to resume their ministries, though this had limited success due, in part, to resistance to such leniency from the Archbishops of Glasgow (Burnet) and St Andrews (Sharp). Nevertheless, around forty ministers did respond and were reinstated. Three years later a further effort was made and another fifty resumed their duties, with more such accommodations following. Alongside such 'carrots' there went a 'stick', namely a tightening of the laws against conventicles and field preaching. These now included the death penalty. Harbouring field preachers also became an offence. Again these policies created division within the covenanting ranks. Some responded positively to the carrots while the rage of others thrived on the sticks. A flashpoint came in 1679 with the assassination of Archbishop Sharp as he journeyed across Magus Muir with his daughter, on their way from Edinburgh to St Andrews. Following this event an attack on a conventicle at Drumclog by a troop of cavalry badly backfired. Their commander, James Graham of Claverhouse, had not made adequate reconnaissance. The Covenanters were well armed and saw off the cavalry. This encouraged a wider rebellion, which was crushed at Bothwell Bridge by a government force led by the Duke of Monmouth, an illegitimate son of Charles II. This resulted in a change at the top of the Scottish government, with James, Duke of York, Charles II's brother, replacing the Duke of Lauderdale as the King's High Commissioner in Scotland. Meantime, in 1681 Charles proceeded to coerce the Scottish Parliament into passing a Test Act that required all holders of office in Church and State to uphold the established order and renounce the Covenants.

It was from such policies that the church body known as the Cameronians emerged. These were the followers of Richard Cameron, who rejected all efforts to find a middle way as sought by Bishop Leighton and others. In addition Cameron absolutely rejected the Catholic James' claim to the throne, even though he was quite legitimately next in line of succession. Charles II had certainly fathered children, though none with his queen; thus his younger brother was next in line. Cameron even went so far as to publicly renounce his allegiance to Charles, branding him a tyrant. Such a challenge could not be ignored, nor was it. So began a period that has, with justification, been branded the 'Killing Time'. Cameron himself was one of the first to die, in a skirmish, and those who succeeded him, Donald Cargill and James Renwick, were eventually caught and executed. Their extremism was not shared by the majority of Presbyterians, but as an ecclesiastical body the Cameronians would continue as one of the strands of Kirk diversity. Known as the Reformed Presbyterian Church, sometimes referred to as Cameronians, the denomination continues to this day, with a presence in a number of countries, including a few congregations in Scotland.

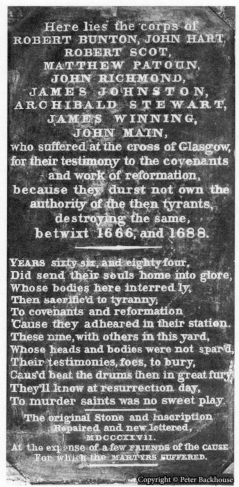

Here lies the corps of
ROBERT BUNTON, JOHN HART,
ROBERT SCOT,
MATTHEW PATOUN,
JOHN RICHMOND,
JAMES JOHNSTON,
ARCHIBALD STEWART,
JAMES WINNING,
JOHN MAIN,
who suffered at the cross of Glasgow,
for their testimony to the covenants
and work of reformation,
because they durst not own the
authority of the then tyrants,
destroying the same,
betwixt 1666, and 1688.

YEARS sixty six, and eighty four,
Did send their souls home into glore,
Whose bodies here interred ly,
Then sacrific'd to tyranny;
To covenants and reformation
'Cause they adheared in their station.
These nine, with others in this yard,
Whose heads and bodies were not spar'd,
Their testimonies, foes, to bury,
Caus'd beat the drums then in great fury,
They'll know at resurrection day,
To murder saints was no sweet play.

The original Stone and Inscription
Repaired and new lettered,
MDCCCXXVII.
At the expense of a few FRIENDS of the CAUSE
For which the MARTYRS SUFFERED.

The Glasgow Covenanters' Memorial.

Charles II died on 6 February 1685 and his brother James duly succeeded to the throne. From the start he was determined to restore Catholicism to his entire kingdom, but soon found he had a fight on his hands. Four years previously the Scottish Parliament had been willing to sign the Test Act, but James was to find it less pliable in 1686 when he sought to repeal the various laws against Catholicism. In the face of growing resistance he persisted in asserting his will as far as he could, thus alienating his subjects north and south of the border. On 10 June 1688 James' second wife, Mary of Modena, gave birth to a son. Named James Francis Edward, he automatically became heir to the throne, displacing his twenty-six-year-old protestant half-sister, Mary, wife of William of Orange. This turn of events, which potentially projected a Catholic succession well into the future, galvanised those determined that this would not happen. By the autumn plans were in place for William to invade, and on 5 November he landed at Brixham in Devon with a significant Dutch force. Almost immediately support for James began to evaporate and on 23 December he fled the country. On 13 February 1689, the English Parliament proclaimed William and Mary as joint sovereigns. The 'Glorious Revolution' had taken place.

In Scotland a Convention of Estates declared the throne vacant and adopted a Claim of Right that narrated various grievances against the policies of James and expressed confidence that William and Mary would respect the religion, laws and liberties of the Scottish people. On this basis the Convention, on 11 April 1689, offered the Scottish throne to William and Mary and issued an edict requiring all ministers to pray for the king and queen. These policies were not unanimously approved, for James had his supporters. These included the bishops, many Highland clans and John Graham of Claverhouse, scourge of the Covenanters and harrier of conventicles such as Drumclog. Claverhouse was a staunch supporter of James who, only the previous November, had conferred upon him the title, Viscount Dundee. Sir Walter Scott captures the moment in his lines:

> To the Lords of Convention 'twas Clavers who spoke,
> 'Ere the king's crown shall fall there are crowns to be broke;
> So let each Cavalier who loves honour and me
> Come follow the bonnet of Bonny Dundee.'

In this mood Claverhouse left the Convention, vowing to summon another, in James' name, to meet in Stirling. Due to vacillation among his supporters this did not happen. Dundee was declared a rebel and on 11 April the Estates offered the Scottish throne to William and Mary. In response Dundee gathered his forces and Scotland found itself, albeit briefly, in another civil war, effectively the first Jacobite rising. The battle came at Killiecrankie at the end of July. The Jacobite forces prevailed though Dundee himself was killed. A month later a close-fought encounter at Dunkeld ended in defeat for the Jacobites at the hands of the Cameronians (poetic justice, some might think), a regiment that took its name from the Covenanter, Richard Cameron.

By then, though, things had moved on politically. In June William had called a Parliament, which proceeded to abolish prelacy and repeal all legislation establishing Episcopacy. Having resolved to remain loyal to the exiled James, the bishops absented themselves from these proceedings. No doubt helped by their absence, the Act of Supremacy, which had declared the Sovereign head of Church as well as State, was repealed and Episcopacy itself was abolished as being 'contrary to the inclinations of the generality of the people'. It is interesting to note the pragmatic as distinct from principled nature of this decision. By these means the way was cleared for the Kirk to be legally established as Presbyterian. Parliament reaffirmed the Act of 1592 declaring church government to be in the hands of Kirk Sessions, Presbyteries, Synods and General Assemblies, and approved the Westminster Confession of Faith as the public Confession of the Church.

A General Assembly met in October 1690. This comprised sixty ministers, ordained before Charles II's re-establishment of Episcopacy in 1662, who were now restored. These became known as the 'antediluvians'. With them were a further fifty-six ministers and forty-six elders. This meant that many of the Church's 900 parishes were not represented. There were also scores to settle from the eviction of non-compliant covenanting ministers and their forced replacement by the derided 'curates'. Such policies continued, though with the boot on the other foot, resulting in 664 ministers being deprived of their charges between 1688 and 1716. Such a troubled background can explain the tone of William's letter to the 1690 Assembly: 'A calm and peaceable procedure will be no less pleasing to us than it becometh you. We could never be of the mind that violence was suited to the advancing of true religion, nor intend that our authority could ever be a tool to the irregular passions of any party. Moderation is what religion enjoins, neighbouring churches expect it and we recommend it to you.' This was entirely in line with the manner in which William had taken the Coronation Oath the previous year. The oath was put to him clause by clause. The last clause called for the king to declare: 'I vow to root out all heretics and enemies to the true worship of God.' William refused, declaring that he would not lay himself under any obligation to be a persecutor.

Amen to that, we might say, but trouble still lay ahead, not least as to how to achieve an accommodation between those who since the 1660s had conformed to the Episcopalian system and those who had resisted. A crucial test was adherence to the Westminster Confession of Faith, beloved by true-blue Presbyterians, while Episcopalians favoured *The Scots Confession* of 1560. The Parliamentary legislation of 1690 referred to the Westminster Confession as 'the public and avowed Confession of this Church, containing the sum and substance of the doctrine of the Reformed Churches' – a fairly broad definition and one around which it might have been possible, through a spirit of good will, for Presbyterians and Episcopalians to coalesce. Two years later this very challenge arose when, with the encouragement of the king, nearly 200 Episcopalian clergy petitioned the General Assembly for admission to the courts of the Church, and indicated a willingness to subscribe the Confession in these terms. King William's letter firmly made the point that the ineligibility of so many serving ministers meant 'that you are not a full General Assembly, there being as great a number of the ministers of the Church of Scotland ... who are not allowed to be represented'. The Assembly responded in time-honoured fashion by setting up a committee. Recognising this as a delaying tactic, the King's Commissioner dissolved the Assembly, a move that, unlike in 1638, was accepted, though not before the Moderator appointed a date for the next Assembly in August 1693. Before that date arrived, however, Parliament passed a piece of legislation the intention of which was made perfectly clear in its title: 'Act of Settling the Quiet and Peace of the Church'. This had two main thrusts. The first was a requirement that all ministers should sign an oath of allegiance to William and Mary, acknowledging their sovereignty in law as well as in fact. Second, the Act provided for the calling of a General Assembly that would include former Episcopalian clergy in the courts of the Church. This raised all the old issues of State interference in church affairs and resulted in anything but quiet and peace. What saved the day was the intervention of another William, William Carstares, Chaplain to the king and a canny Scot, who persuaded his majesty not to make the taking of a civil oath a condition of holding office as a minister. Carstares had travelled with William from Holland in 1688 and would go on to become minister of Greyfriars, then of St Giles', Principal of Edinburgh University and Moderator of the General Assembly.

However, the position of Episcopalian clergy in church courts remained unresolved. Indeed, the entirely Presbyterian Assembly of 1693 decided to tighten the terms of adherence to the Westminster Confession beyond the formula indicated in the Act of Parliament. The 1693 terms of subscription were: 'I sincerely own and declare the Confession of Faith ... to be the confession of my faith; and that I own the doctrine therein contained to be the true doctrine which I will constantly adhere to.' It was as if the Presbyterian majority was setting up the Confession as a standard higher even than Scripture, and the predictable outcome was the continuing exclusion from the courts of the Church of those who had conformed to pre-1690 Episcopalian requirements. These Episcopalians were prepared to acknowledge the Confession as a 'sum and substance of the faith of the Church', but to be required to own it in every particular as a statement of their own personal belief was another matter. In the event Parliament protected their right to continue their ministries within their charges. It is recorded that 165 such ministers were serving on this basis in 1707. Indeed, Archibald Lundie of Saltoun served his parish from 1696 to 1759 without ever subscribing the Westminster Confession or participating in the courts of the Church. This achievement earned him the title, 'the last of the old Scotch Episcopalians'. There was, though, a real sadness in all of this. In practice Presbyterian and Episcopalian forms of worship were largely indistinguishable and doctrinally the mainline adherents of both systems had much in common. What separated them was a disagreement over aspects of church government and the manner of adherence to the Confession of Faith.

Witchcraft and Blasphemy

There is a maxim that the first casualty of war is truth. Each side will claim all the virtue and attribute all the evil to their opponent. Sadly, if inevitably, Britain's sixteenth- and seventeenth-century religious struggles sometimes led to war and, even after an interval of three centuries, the temptation faced by a narrator of these events is to attribute, if not all, at least more fault to one side rather than the other. Biographies of religious leaders of the past can too readily slip into hagiography or demonisation, depending on the viewpoint of the author. At the same time, care has to be taken not to judge the past and those who inhabited it by the standards of the present. As L. P. Hartley famously put it: 'the past is a foreign country; they do things differently there'. That said, the fact remains that in any conflict there are faults on both sides – trite but true – and an account of Scottish church history that suggests otherwise will not be faithful to the facts. There were good and bad Catholics, good and bad Protestants; good and bad Episcopalians, good and bad Presbyterians; and the stories that follow, from the aftermath of the 1690 Presbyterian settlement, do not show the Kirk in a good light.

Christian Shaw was the daughter of John Shaw, Laird of Bargrennan in Renfrewshire. When she was eleven years old she caught a housemaid, Catherine Campbell, helping herself to milk without permission. Christian reported the offence to her mother and Catherine responded angrily, cursing the child with the words 'The Devil hurl (throw) your soul through hell.' Shortly afterwards Christian started having fits. Pinch marks appeared on her body. It was claimed that she even floated around rooms without touching the floor. Her father sought medical advice and her condition was diagnosed as demonic possession. Christian began to name names of those who had tormented her. Arrests were made and twenty-one people were subjected to tests by 'witch prickers', seeking the 'numb spot' or a claw-shaped mark on their bodies, which indicated their guilt.

The case eventually came to trial at Paisley under a 1563 Act of Parliament anent Witchcraft, Sorcery and Necromancy. Prior to the hearing the Revd James Hutcheson, minister at Killallan, preached before the judges. He took as his text Exodus 22:18: 'Thou shalt not suffer a witch to live' and cited various texts he deemed relevant to the matter in hand. In the event, fourteen of those rounded up were found not guilty and released. The remaining seven, including the maid, Catherine Campbell, were sentenced to death. On 10 June 1697 a gibbet was set up and a fire kindled on Paisley's Gallow Green. Those condemned were executed in a most brutal and barbaric manner – hanged, cut down while still alive, then burned in the fire. Knowing what fate awaited him, one escaped execution, but only by hanging himself in his cell the night before. Of course, the word went around that he had been hanged by the devil. It was also reported that after these proceedings there were no recurrences of Christian Shaw's bizarre behaviour or symptoms. The case was not unique, though the times were slowly changing. In 1727, Janet Horne of Dornoch became the last person to be executed as a witch, and the 1563 Act was finally repealed in 1735. John Buchan's novel, *Witch Wood*, offers a fictional yet historically credible account of a mid-seventeenth-century minister, the Revd David Sempill, and his dealings with parishioners and fellow presbyters, including an investigation of alleged witchcraft.

Another horror story from 1697 concerned a twenty-one-year-old student, Thomas Aikenhead, the son of an Edinburgh surgeon, who was executed for blasphemy.

During the General Assembly of 1696, concerns had been expressed over the propagation of atheistic teaching. Unfortunately for young Thomas, he had drawn attention to himself by maintaining that 'theology was a rhapsody of ill-feigned nonsense'. In addition he had referred to the Old Testament as 'Ezra's fables' and the New Testament as 'the history of the impostor Christ'. As if this were not enough, he had predicted the demise of Christianity by the year 1800. On the basis of these views, publicly expressed, he was charged with blasphemy in December 1696.

At his trial he admitted having made the offending statements but said he was simply quoting from books he had read – books of the sort, presumably, that had troubled the Assembly earlier in the year. Thomas insisted that he did not personally believe such things; on the contrary he affirmed his adherence to 'the Protestant religion', begged for mercy and resolved, if spared, to demonstrate throughout the rest of his life his abhorrence of the views he had rashly expressed. It was to no avail.

On Christmas Eve he was sentenced to death. A petition was submitted to the Privy Council asking that consideration be given to his 'deplorable circumstances and tender years'. The appeal further pointed out that his defence had failed to mention that he was a first-time offender. To their credit two ministers and two Privy Councillors pleaded on his behalf, but to no avail. On 7 January, after another petition, the Privy Council ruled that they would not grant a reprieve unless the Church interceded for him. The General Assembly, sitting in Edinburgh at the time, was duly approached. Their response was to urge 'vigorous execution' to curb 'the abounding of impiety and profanity in this land'. On 8 January the sentence was carried out – the last execution for blasphemy in Britain.

The Barrier Act

We conclude this chapter on the seventeenth century with a further reference to the business of the General Assembly in January 1697.

It is an established principle of Reformed Churches that Reformation is not a once and for all event. Rather it is a continuing process. This is traditionally expressed in a Latin phrase: *ecclesia reformata semper reformanda* – a Church reformed and in continuing need of reform. And yet, having come through all the struggles of the Reformation period, and looking back and counting the cost, there was an understandable concern to protect what had been achieved and secure it against backsliding or ill-considered change. To this end the General Assembly of 1697 (as it happened, on the very day of Thomas Aikenhead's execution) passed a measure entitled 'Act anent the Method of passing Acts of Assembly of general concern to the Church, and for the preventing of Innovations'. This measure, known as the Barrier Act, remains in force to this day. Essentially, it ensures that any proposed changes in the areas of church worship, government, doctrine or discipline must first be adopted by the General Assembly and then sent to presbyteries for their consideration. Only if a majority of presbyteries approve may the next Assembly pass the changes into law. There are two further requirements: First, the assent must come from a majority of all presbyteries, not just of those sending in a return; second, even if the required presbytery support is forthcoming the subsequent Assembly may still decline to give final approval.

As the title indicates, the purpose of the Act is to prevent hasty and ill-considered change, but also to ensure that laws, once passed, are respected and obeyed. It can also be noted that the Barrier Act itself complied with its own procedures. Before being approved in 1697 it had been presented as an Overture to the 1696 Assembly and received the support of a majority of presbyteries. These, of course, were presbyteries that, like the

Assembly itself, comprised only ministers who had subscribed the Westminster Confession, thereby excluding many who had been prepared to serve under the period of Episcopal church government prior to 1690. The Act itself is not part of the Church's constitution, though in practice a General Assembly faced with a proposal to amend or repeal it would in all likelihood decide to send the proposals for the consideration of presbyteries under the Act.

THE EIGHTEENTH CENTURY

The Presbyterian Settlement Challenged

The new century was little over a year old when, on 8 March 1702, King William died. Queen Mary had predeceased him in December 1694. As they had no children, the Crown passed to Mary's younger sister, Anne. It is recorded that, when informed of her accession by William's Chaplain, Bishop Burnet of Salisbury, Queen Anne was at a loss for words and could respond only by talking about the weather. Looking out of the window she remarked: 'It is a fine day.' The bishop, well schooled in courtly manners, is said to have replied: 'The finest day that ever dawned for England, ma'am.'

In passing it is interesting to note that the Edinburgh, born Gilbert Burnet was a nephew of Archibald Johnston of Warriston, one of the drafters of the National Covenant. Burnet had begun his ministry in Scotland, serving at East Saltoun from 1665 to 1669. From there he moved to the Chair of Divinity at Glasgow University, but after five years he had had enough of Scotland's turbulent church politics and moved to London. With such a Scottish pedigree, why did his flattery of the new queen refer to the finest day that ever dawned for England? Had a quarter century of Anglicanism led him to use 'England' to refer to the entirety of Great Britain? Or was his language not so much courtly as perceptive? Just fourteen years after the Glorious Revolution, was there a possibility that things might unravel north of the border? The exiled James VII and II had died six months before William, but he had left a teenage son, also named James, who would become known as the 'Old Pretender' (claimant) to the throne. In the event James bided his time until after Anne's death in 1714. Nevertheless, his very existence, with French and Episcopal support, had the capacity to rock the ship of state; and evidence of such concerns soon emerged.

The 1690s had been a difficult decade for Scotland. The infamous Massacre of Glencoe in February 1692 was a deeply unsettling event. The clan chief of the Macdonalds had failed to take an oath of allegiance to King William by the due date, and the king's Scottish advisers saw the opportunity to teach the highlanders a lesson. They persuaded William to sign an order for the 'extirpation of that sect of thieves', and the resultant massacre created widespread outrage, readily seized upon by Jacobite sympathisers to discredit the king. The 1690s also saw 'seven ill years', which brought widespread crop failures, leading to famine and further deterioration in the nation's fragile economic position. This had led some to call for a political union with England, but other and stronger voices had preferred policies for developing Scottish trade as the way to get the country back on its feet. This latter feeling prevailed and in 1695 the Scottish Parliament established the Bank of Scotland and a Company of Scotland with authority to raise capital to finance trading with Africa and the Indies. Funds were duly raised in London, Hamburg and Amsterdam but English commercial interests, such as the East India Company, felt threatened by these moves and successfully applied pressure on investors to withdraw their funds. As a result, plans to trade with Africa and the Indies were abandoned and an alternative scheme was adopted. This was to develop a Scots trading colony on the Gulf of Darien in Panama and establish a land route between the Atlantic and Pacific. Forced back on their own resources the Scots raised the sum of £400,000 for the project – the equivalent of £47 million today and a sum representing one-fifth of the nation's wealth. However, diplomatic considerations came into play alongside political and economic ones. Panama lay within territory claimed by Spain as its colony of New Granada. England was at war with France and King William had no wish to alienate Spain as well. Accordingly, his support of the Darien Scheme was at best lukewarm. Nevertheless, it went ahead, with disastrous consequences in terms of life and fortune for colonists, investors and the Scottish nation as a whole.

It is not difficult to see why the Scots blamed their southern neighbour and their shared king for this outcome. In 1703 the Scottish Parliament responded by passing an Act anent Peace and War, which asserted Scotland's right to pursue a different foreign policy from England. Then, in defiance of the Duke of Queensberry, Queen Anne's Commissioner in Scotland, Parliament passed an Act of Security. This reserved Scotland's right to choose its own successor to Queen Anne unless certain conditions were met. These conditions included 'free communication of trade ... and the liberty of the plantations'; also a requirement that 'there be such conditions of government settled and enacted as may secure ... the freedom, frequency and the power of Parliament, and the religion, liberty and trade of the nation from English and foreign influence.' In 1705 the English Parliament retaliated with the Alien Act. This declared that until Scotland accepted the Hanoverian succession, all Scots would be treated as aliens in England and the import of Scottish sheep, cattle, coal and linen would not be allowed. None of this was helpful to either nation and, increasingly, parliamentary union appeared to be the only way of resolving the deepening crisis.

However, for the Kirk and many Scots such a union was a less than welcome step beyond the union of Crowns. Under James and his successors that earlier union had resulted in a bitter struggle between presbytery and bishop that had, on occasions, been fought out on the field of battle. As long as Scotland had its own Parliament, the Kirk might reasonably expect to retain its influence on public policy, an influence that would be at best marginal in a London-based Parliament.

In the century and more since the Reformation, the Kirk's position had certainly waxed and waned. In 1567, after the forced abdication of Mary Queen of Scots, the Scottish Parliament had ratified and confirmed the legislation of 1560 and established the Scottish Church as Reformed and Protestant. One of the chief Acts passed by that Parliament had declared: 'there is no other face of Kirk nor other face of Religion than is presently by the favour God established within this Realm'. Another Act of the same Parliament required the monarch to root out all opposed to the Church's teaching. Further legislation of 1579 referred to the Kirk as 'the only true and holy Kirk of Jesus Christ within this realm'. There had then followed a century of bitter strife, but the 1690 settlement had consolidated that earlier position. From the Presbyterian point of view this was very positive. At the same time, and given past experience, there was a natural concern to secure these arrangements in any parliamentary union with England.

This desire found expression in a number of ways. A 1705 Act of the Scottish Parliament specifically stated that those appointed to negotiate with English parliamentarians 'shall not treat of, or concerning, any alteration of the worship, discipline and government of the Church of this kingdom as now by law established'. An equivalent measure was adopted by the English Parliament in respect of the Church of England. The following year the Scottish Parliament passed the Protestant Religion and Presbyterian Church Act, which became known as (another) Act of Security. This declared that the queen 'with the advice and consent of the said Estates of Parliament, doth herby establish and confirm the true Protestant Religion and Worship, Discipline and Government of the Church to continue without any alteration to the people in this land in succeeding generations'. Again, equivalent legislative assurances were provided for the Church of England and these were included alongside the 1707 Treaty of Union. The union also settled the British succession on Sophia, the Electress of Hanover, and provided for free trade both within Great Britain and with England's foreign possessions. To this day the Sovereign's letter, read out at the opening of the General Assembly, concludes with a pledge to maintain and preserve the Protestant Religion and Presbyterian church government in Scotland, the pledge itself being incorporated into the Accession Oath. With such assurances things looked set fair for the Kirk's security within the unified state of Great Britain. Within a very short time, however, its position would be challenged, successfully.

In 1709 the Reverend James Greenshields, an Episcopalian minister, opened a meeting house in premises in Edinburgh near to St Giles', and conducted services using the Anglican Book of Common Prayer. This was allowed on the basis that he had taken an oath of loyalty to Queen Anne and prayed for her in his services. This was essential given that Episcopalians were suspected of Jacobite sympathies. However, his landlord demurred and took steps to have Greenshields evicted. Undaunted, he soon found alternative accommodation and continued with his services. The Presbytery of Edinburgh then intervened and instructed him to stop. Not unreasonably Greenshields pointed out that as he was not one of their ministers, he was not subject to their authority. The Presbytery then involved the magistrates, who interpreted the 1690 Presbyterian settlement as ruling out any other form of worship, so there was no need for a specific law 'condemning the English service'. Not only did the magistrates find against Greenshields, they committed him to the Tolbooth prison. The case then made its way to the Court of Session, which upheld the judgement of the magistrates, adding that Greenshields would remain in prison until he promised to abandon his services. This he refused to do, for he had other plans and clever advisers. Taking advantage of the recent union of Parliaments he appealed to the House of Lords in London. There his case was heard sympathetically and, after a year of languishing in the Tolbooth, he was released and allowed to continue his ministry unmolested. He was even awarded damages against the magistrates.

This House of Lords judgement was a game-changer. The year 1710 had brought to power a high Tory Government that was strongly sympathetic to Episcopalianism. Greenshields' success was soon followed by an 'Act to prevent the Disturbing those of Episcopal Communion in that part of Great Britain called Scotland in the exercise of their religious worship and in the use of the liturgy of the Church of England.' Known more briefly as the Act of Toleration, this meant that Episcopalian clergy were now free to conduct services using the English Prayer Book, provided they pledged allegiance to Queen Anne and renounced any commitment to Jacobitism. A bar on their baptising children and solemnising marriages was also removed. This was a major blow to the Presbyterian monopoly, though it also had damaging consequences for the Episcopal Church. Not all of their clergy took the oath and so they became divided into jurors and non-jurors, the latter adhering to the Jacobite cause. The Kirk protested, to no avail. Nevertheless, it did retain some of its rights and privileges, even though a major blow had been struck against the principle of 'no other face of Kirk nor other face of Religion'. The new Episcopal Church legislation declared 'that nothing herein contained shall be construed to exempt any of the persons frequenting the said Episcopal congregations from paying of tithes or other parochial duties to the church or minister of the parish to which they belong or in which they reside'. The Act also required that a record of Episcopalian Baptisms be kept in the Parish register and that banns of marriage in respect of Episcopal ceremonies also be called in the parish church.

With the bit well and truly between its teeth the London government proceeded to deliver a further and far more serious blow to the Kirk by passing the Church Patronage Act. Patronage was the right of landowners, town councils and other bodies to nominate and, effectively, appoint ministers to vacant churches. It had been abolished as part of the 1690 settlement in recognition of a congregation's right to choose its minister; but now the London Parliament was restoring that right to patrons. This was contrary to the 1705 Act of Security, which had been incorporated into the Act of Union. The General Assembly protested but to no effect. Parliament was a long way off and Scotland had only one more member there than Cornwall.

Royal Arms of Great Britain (1736) and Robert Burns Memorial Window (1985), St Giles' Cathedral.

In 1714 Queen Anne died and the House of Stewart gave way to the House of Hanover. As Princess Sophia had died a few weeks before Queen Anne, her son succeeded to the throne as George I. He was a great-grandson on his mother's side of James VI and I and thus in direct line of succession to the thrones of both Scotland and England. So also was the Catholic James, the 'Old Pretender', and the following year would see a new Jacobite rising on his behalf.

Theological Tensions

While external forces were thus threatening the 1690 Presbyterian settlement, the Church's internal unity and coherence was also at risk through theological differences.

In the General Assembly of 1714 there was a move to inquire into the teaching of Dr John Simson, Professor of

Divinity at Glasgow University. The matter dragged on for some years but, essentially, Professor Simson was accused of teaching 'that it is possible that none are excluded from the benefit of the remedy for sin provided by God', an opinion that flew in the face of the doctrine of predestination. It was not easy to prove that Simson had actually taught what was alleged. The witnesses were mainly his students and, in those days, professors delivered their lectures in Latin, a language in which not all students were highly proficient. Eventually, the General Assembly of 1717 held that Simson 'had vented some opinions not necessary to be taught in divinity' and took no further action. In 1725 there was further controversy, this time suggesting that Simson was questioning the divinity of Christ. Again the matter was investigated, leading eventually to his suspension by the Assembly of 1728. There it was held that his teaching was subversive and his explanations tardy, albeit his 'sentiments' were judged 'sound and orthodox'. The matter was also referred to presbyteries, where pressure was growing for Simson's removal from all ecclesiastical functions. This indeed was what happened the following year, though notwithstanding the Assembly's judgement that he was not 'fit or safe' to teach divinity, Simson was allowed to retain the emoluments of the Chair. The case clearly exposed tensions within the Church as to what extent free and original thinking might have its place.

Around this time another controversy arose over what became known as the 'Auchterarder Creed'. The Presbytery of Auchterarder, with a view to encouraging a more evangelical form of Calvinism, drew up certain questions to be put to those seeking acceptance for training for the ministry. In particular such candidates were required to affirm: 'I believe that it is not sound and orthodox to teach that we must forsake sin, in order to our coming to Christ and instating us in covenant with God.' This rather clumsy declaration was simply seeking an assurance that a candidate held that Christ accepts people as sinners. Simple enough, perhaps, but one such candidate,

William Craig, declined to give his assent and challenged the Presbytery's right to impose any test beyond the official formula of subscription to the Westminster Confession of Faith. He appealed to the General Assembly, which supported his position and instructed the Presbytery to allow him to proceed to the ministry. However, the Assembly did not leave it at that; rather, it went on to condemn not only the procedure of the Presbytery in imposing its own test, but also the 'Auchterarder Creed' as tending 'to encourage people's sloth as Christians and slacken people's obligation to Gospel holiness'. As it happened, this was the same Assembly that declined to take action against Professor Simson's alleged undermining of the Westminster Confession. Now it appeared to be denouncing a presbytery that considered it was doing no more than reaffirming the Confession's teaching.

There is a third ingredient to these theological disputes, namely what became known as the 'Marrow' controversy. In 1646 a book entitled *The Marrow of Modern Divinity* had been published in England. This was in the form of a dialogue involving a minister named Evangelista, a young Christian called Neophytes, a legalist, appropriately named Nomista, who believes Christianity is a set of rules to be obeyed (*nomos* is the Greek word for 'law') and Antinomista, who thinks it's all right to sin because God, in his mercy, will forgive you anyway. The conclusion of the dialogue is an assertion of the centrality of faith and the sufficiency of grace for salvation.

One of those particularly offended by the manner in which the General Assembly had dealt with the Simson and Auchterarder cases was Thomas Boston, minister at Simprin in Berwickshire. In his view the Assembly had been too lenient with Simson and unnecessarily harsh with the Presbytery of Auchterarder. It so happened that around this time a parishioner had given him a copy of the largely forgotten *Marrow* and he had been much taken with it; so much so that in 1718, along with Thomas Hog of Carnock, he published a new edition with a preface warmly commending its teaching. This created both interest and controversy, for it was not long before others were condemning the book. The following year James Hadow, Principal of St Mary's College, St Andrews, preached at the Synod of Fife against what he referred to as the *Marrow*'s 'antinomian' tendencies. Essentially, 'antinomianism' argued that since Christians are saved by faith in Christ, good works are irrelevant to salvation. Hadow's sermon was subsequently published under the title *The Record of God and the Duty of Faith therein required*. The very title highlights the issue. Salvation may indeed be the gift of a gracious God, but its acceptance calls for a response in dutiful lives that are changed by divine grace. The sermon prompted an exchange of pamphlets and, with Boston and Hog claiming they had been misrepresented, the Assembly of 1719 remitted the whole matter to its Committee for Purity of Doctrine. The following year the Committee declared the *Marrow* indeed to be antinomian, and this view received strong backing from the Assembly. The book was condemned and ministers were instructed to warn their congregations against reading it, an outcome that, predictably, led to a surge in sales. This, though, was not the end of the matter. The following year twelve ministers, including Boston, Hogg and two brothers, Ebenezer and Ralph Erskine, brought a 'Representation and Petition' in which they maintained that, in condemning the *Marrow*, the Assembly had condemned propositions that were entirely Scriptural, along with other thoroughly orthodox beliefs. The Assembly rejected these claims, reaffirmed its condemnation of the *Marrow* and issued a stern rebuke to the petitioners.

To the modern mind these eighteenth-century disputes feel quite divorced from real life, casting the General Assembly as little more than a talking shop convened for the purpose of debating abstruse points of academic theology. It was as though, having emerged from a century of post-Reformation struggle with a significant Presbyterian settlement and weathered the external challenges of the London government, the Church was now turning in on itself. There were two camps: those comfortable with inherited traditions and others who sensed that attitudes were changing and welcomed the challenge this brought. For the latter group, Christianity was more than academic argument over the relationship between belief and practice. Rather it was about engagement with the world of new ideas and the bringing to bear of the Gospel upon that world in ways that related to it. It was alleged that Professor Simson, whose 'heretical' views started the whole thing off, even considered that there might be people living on the moon. This certainly suggests an inquiring mind and Simson had his supporters and admirers. Indeed, one of his students, Francis Hutcheson, went on to become Professor of Moral Philosophy at Glasgow University and one of the leading figures in the Scottish Enlightenment. Simson may have been less than candid when questioned by the Committee on the Purity of Doctrine but his thinking clearly went well beyond the range of that Committee's interests.

Tensions become Divisions

A recurring theme in any account of the Kirk over the centuries is the matter of patronage, abolished as part of the 1690 settlement, reimposed following the Union of Parliaments and one of the primary issues that would lead to the Disruption of 1843. In the period currently under consideration there were those who considered that, as patronage was the law of the land, the Church just had to get on with it. There were certainly patrons who sought to present ministers who would be acceptable to the people. Such efforts, though, were often in vain since for some the nomination of the archangel Gabriel himself would have been unacceptable simply by dint of being the patron's choice. So clashes arose as congregations appealed to presbyteries not to induct the nominee. Sometimes such appeals succeeded, sometimes not. Paradoxically, the General Assembly annually protested the iniquity of the system to Parliament, while vigorously enforcing the policy. One method of enforcement was the 'riding committee', charged with carrying through the induction when a presbytery was unwilling to do so. (The term 'riding' might suggest either or both of the overriding of the congregation's wishes, or the dispatch of a mounted clerical posse to ensure compliance with the law.) As might be anticipated, such proceedings were carried through with less than dignity. At least one unwanted presentee ended up in a duck pond. That was at New Machar in 1729, but such disputed presentations continued throughout the century. In 1773 the Presbytery of Stirling, under instruction from the General Assembly, reluctantly convened to induct a minister to the charge of St Ninian's in face of opposition sustained over a period of seven years from 600 heads of families and the great majority of the kirk session. In the almost empty church the Moderator referred to the inductee as a 'stipend lifter' and urged him to think again as he had no prospect of an effective ministry. His terse response was to tell the Moderator to 'proceed to execute the instructions of your superiors'.

Clearly, this kind of situation was far from satisfactory, and in 1731 the General Assembly took steps to find, if not a solution, at least some compromise. Closer scrutiny of the law revealed that the patron's right of presentation had to be exercised within six months of the vacancy arising, failing which the right of appointment devolved to the presbytery. When this situation arose the presbytery would normally consult the local elders before proceeding. A refinement of this arrangement was adopted by the General Assembly of 1731 and sent to presbyteries for their views under the Barrier Act. The proposal was that where the patron had failed to act within six months, the right of nomination should lie with the elders and Protestant heritors (feudal landowners) in country parishes, and the elders and town councils in burghs. The Assembly further advised that, if presbyteries failed to express an opinion, the measure would be adopted by the subsequent Assembly. The following year it was reported that thirty-one presbyteries were opposed to the proposal, arguing strongly for full congregational right of nomination and call. Only six were in favour, with a further twelve prepared to agree if certain changes were made. Eighteen presbyteries made no response and, true to the heavy hint of the previous year, the Assembly presumed these to be in favour (or at least not opposed), added them to the six and twelve and declared the measure carried.

Later that year at a meeting of the Synod of Perth and Stirling, the Synod Moderator, Ebenezer Erskine, condemned these Assembly proceedings and reaffirmed the congregation's right of call as a principle going back to the *Books of Discipline*. The following April the Synod met again and Erskine was urged to retract his criticism, which he refused to do and, in consequence, found himself summoned to appear before the following month's General Assembly. When called, Erskine handed in a written protest and demanded that its contents be minuted. This was refused but, somehow, the paper fluttered to the floor, where it was picked up and perused by James Naismith, minister at Dalmeny. He was so outraged by what he read that he interrupted proceedings, asking that the Assembly consider the insults contained in the Protest. Erskine was summoned to re-appear the following day and ordered to apologise, failing which he and three supporting colleagues would be suspended from the ministry. The colleagues were William Wilson, minister at Perth, Alexander Moncrieff, minister at Abernethy and James Fisher, minister at Kinclaven. Wisely a pause was interposed and the matter was remitted to a Commission of Assembly, a body comprising a proportion of the membership of the Assembly with delegated powers. When the matter came before the Commission a motion to delay any suspension of the four received an equal number of votes for and against, but was lost on the casting vote of the Moderator. Notwithstanding, further efforts at reconciliation were made, but when these finally broke down the decision to suspend was taken by a large majority.

The response of the four was to publish a document, dated 16 November 1733, asserting their Presbyterian principles and claiming that they were not seceding from the Church but from 'the prevailing party' within it, whom they maintained were 'carrying on a course of defection from our Reformed and Covenanted principles'. On 1 December they met at Gairney Bridge in Kinross-shire and constituted themselves 'The Associate Presbytery'. Though only four in number this was a significant secession, and before very long the Kirk realised it had not handled the matter well. The General Assembly of 1734 repealed the legislation that had forced the seceders' hand and even instructed the Synod of Perth and Stirling to receive them back into the ministry. However, by then they had published their Testimony and four more ministers had joined them, including Ralph Erskine, brother of Ebenezer. They began to organise, establishing churches around the country, exercising judicial functions and appointing William Wilson as Professor of Divinity. Throughout this period they were permitted to remain in their manses and receive their stipends but the Kirk's belated 'softly, softly' approach was of no avail. The damage had been done and the new denomination was proving popular, particularly among working people. Finally, in 1740, the seceding ministers were deposed and by 1745 the Secession Church had forty-five congregations.

There is a story told of a Scottish Presbyterian who was shipwrecked and found refuge on a desert island. Eventually he was rescued when a passing ship responded to signals from the island. He had kept himself occupied during his time as a castaway but what particularly caught the attention of his rescuers was that he had built not one but two churches. 'Why two?' they enquired. 'Well,' he explained, pointing to each in turn, 'that's the one I go to and that's the one I don't go to on principle.' What follows illustrates why such a story could gain traction.

The year 1745 was significant in Scottish history, with

another Jacobite rising in support of Charles Edward Stewart, known to history as Bonnie Prince Charlie or the 'Young Pretender'. The rising ended at Culloden in April 1746, finally laying to rest any prospect of a Stewart monarch returning to the throne. In response to the Jacobite threat the government introduced what became known as the Burgess Oath. Burgesses (citizens) of Edinburgh, Glasgow and Perth were all required to swear the oath that was in these terms: 'Here I protest before God, and your Lordships, that I profess and allow with all my heart the true religion presently professed within this realm and authorised by the laws thereof: I shall abide thereat and defend the same to my life's end, renouncing the Roman religion called Papistry.' Non-subscribers would forfeit the right to vote, enter a trade guild or conduct business. Loyal Protestant citizens should have no scruples over signing and so have nothing to fear.

For the Seceders, though, it wasn't quite as simple as that. What was meant by 'the true religion professed within this realm'? Was it simply Presbyterianism or was it Presbyterianism as represented by the Established Church from which they had so bitterly parted company? If the former, subscription would not be a problem; if the latter, it would be unthinkable. Fierce debate ensued as to whether the taking of the oath was consistent with their principles, and the outcome, in 1747, was a split within the Secession. 'Burghers' (as they became known) were content to take the oath; 'Anti-Burghers' were not. This latter group held the oath to imply 'immediate and full communion with the present Established Church' and 'a solemn abjuration of the whole Secession Testimony'. What started out as a difference of opinion soon developed into fierce disagreement, division, recrimination and, ultimately, separation.

Overtures were made by the Burgher party with a view to healing the breach, but these were rejected. The Anti-Burghers were implacable and proceeded against their former colleagues, even purporting, initially, to depose them from the ministry and, subsequently, to excommunicate them. The rhetoric was certainly ramped up. For interpreting the oath as not inconsistent with Secession principles the Burghers were denounced by their former colleagues as 'those whom the Lord Jesus commands to be holden by … the faithful as heathen men and publicans'. The leader of the Anti-Burgher faction was a man called Adam Gib, who was reputed to have signed a covenant with God in his own blood. His name lingers on in a pend called Gibb's (sic) Entry, off Nicolson Street on the south side of Edinburgh, near to the site where his church once stood.

The controversy was not without its effect on family life. Ebenezer Erskine's daughter, Ailie, was married to James Scott, minister at Gateshaw, near Kelso. Erskine took the Burgher line, while his son-in-law was an Anti-Burgher. It is recorded that when Scott returned home from the Synod that had excommunicated the Erskines and broke the news to his wife, she responded: 'You have excommunicated my father and my uncle! You are my husband, but never more shall you be minister of mine.' She was as good as her word, thereafter riding each Sunday to church in Jedburgh.

Scotland now had three Presbyterian denominations – the Established Church and two Seceder factions. It was soon to have a fourth, but before proceeding to that saga we will take a break from debates and divisions in Presbytery and General Assembly and consider how things stood at the congregational level.

Evangelism and Congregational Life

An insight into the Seceder mindset can be gauged from their treatment of the English evangelist, George Whitfield. In 1741, following Whitfield's successes in North America, Ralph Erskine invited him to visit Scotland. At the same time he took the opportunity to outline Secession principles and inform Whitfield of the way they had been treated by the Established Church. The invitation also made clear that Whitfield's evangelistic endeavours should be restricted to the Seceders and that he should have no dealings with the 'corrupt clergy', who were carrying on 'a course of defection'. Whitfield accepted Erskine's invitation and preached in his church in Dunfermline but, in doing so, made it very clear that he would preach the Gospel to all who would listen, regardless of denomination. This did not play well with the Seceders who, following some heated exchanges, dismissed him as 'a wild enthusiast who was engaged in doing the work of Satan'. Shaking the Seceder dust from his shoes, Whitfield proceeded to preach in the open, attracting great crowds as he went.

In the same year (1741) a lengthy and disputed vacancy in Cambuslang was finally filled by a minister entirely acceptable to the congregation. His name was William McCulloch and he had a son who was a trader in the North American colonies. From this son and other Glasgow-based merchants, McCulloch learned of religious revivals in New England. Greatly inspired, he began to share letters describing these events with members of his congregation. As a result, many became enthused and began to hold evangelical meetings, where they would lament their sins and seek assurance of salvation. These were highly emotional affairs and the gatherings continued over several months. News travels and, on learning of these developments, Whitfield decided to see for himself and travelled to Cambuslang. There, in June 1742, he preached to a crowd numbering some 30,000, gathered on a hillside known as the 'preaching braes'. There, following the sermon, around 3,000 people received Holy Communion. These happenings became known as the 'Cambuslang Wark' (work), and similar revivalist gatherings took place at Kilsyth and elsewhere, albeit on a lesser scale. In all Whitfield paid fourteen visits to Scotland between 1741 and 1768, where he was a welcome guest in pulpits of the evangelical wing of the Kirk.

John Wesley also saw Scotland as a mission field, visiting no fewer than twenty-two times between 1751 and 1790. It was said that he travelled 5,000 miles a year and delivered fifteen sermons a week, and he lived up to this reputation. He certainly covered the ground, preaching in various towns, including Glasgow, Aberdeen, Inverness, Arbroath, Annan and Portpatrick, though with less success than Whitfield. It is further recorded that Wesley attended a session of the General Assembly and observed a case concerning the disputed move of a minister from one parish to another. The matter took five hours to reach a conclusion, at which point Wesley was heard to remark that it could have been resolved in five minutes!

Reference has already been made to patterns of worship following the Reformation. We have also seen how the seventeenth-century Kirk swung between Presbyterianism and Episcopalianism. Against this background it is worth remarking that at local level there was very little difference between the two forms of worship. Before the arrival of the minister the Presbyterian service began with the precentor leading the singing of a psalm; in the Episcopal service he read passages of Scripture. Episcopalians recited the Lord's Prayer, while the Presbyterians, regarding such practice as vain repetition, did not. In services of Baptism, Episcopalians required the father to recite the Apostles' Creed, while Presbyterians sought his assent to the Confession of Faith. Both persuasions believed in extempore prayer and served the Sacrament to the people seated at long tables, these having first been 'fenced'. This 'fencing of the table' was the term used to describe an additional sermon, preached to each sitting of communicants, warning of the danger of eating and drinking unworthily. This was really a final warning since nobody would get near the table in the first place without having been issued with a token of their worthiness signifying a successful outcome of a rigorous examination by the minister or elder of each individual's personal life. The communion card, which survives to this day in some congregations, is a reminder of this practice. The elders themselves were not exempt. As a Communion season approached, a kirk session meeting would be held at which each elder in turn would leave the room while those remaining would inquire of each other whether they had heard of any scandal concerning their brother. Even in church government there was little outward difference between the Presbytery, with its oversight of the ministers, and the Episcopal Synod, chaired by the bishop, in its oversight of the clergy.

Ministers were provided with manses that were typically modest, thatch-roofed homes, and stipend was often paid in kind as well as cash. The eighteenth-century minister's duties involved regular visitation, often combined with catechising and examining the people in their knowledge of the Bible and the catechisms. Kirk session meetings had a strong disciplinary role, with parishioners summoned to appear to answer allegations of misbehaviour. These might range from adultery to minor failures in Sabbath observance. Sometimes cases could ascend to the higher level of Presbytery, which was also the court before which allegations against ministers were heard, often at considerable length.

Church buildings were generally not in a good state of repair and heritors were slow to exercise their responsibility in this regard. Statistical Accounts written by parish ministers use terms such as 'gloomy', 'ruinous', 'filthy and out of repair'. There were even situations where the buried bones of former parishioners protruded through the earthen floor. Temples of beauty to the glory of God they were not. For example, the minister of Glenorchy, writing in 1792, sums up the situation: 'many of our country kirks are such dark, damp, dirty hovels as to chill and repulse every sentiment of devotion; they besides endanger the health of every class of worshipper and encourage the indolent and indifferent in their negligence of instruction'. Yet these were the surroundings in which people were expected to spend many hours on a Sunday, morning and afternoon, listening to lengthy sermons often preached on the same text for weeks on end, with a catechising of young people for 'entertainment' as they shared their meagre lunch.

'Entertainment' was also available through the notorious

rebuking stool on which gossipers, fornicators and Sabbath breakers were made to perch while being given a public dressing down by the minister. For many this was the high point of the service. In his novel, *Annals of the Parish*, John Galt offers a whimsical account of such proceedings when the hero of his novel, the Revd Micah Balwhidder, himself becomes the subject of gossip. Some months after the death of the first Mrs Balwhidder, one of the manse servant girls becomes pregnant. The risk to the minister's reputation energises the inquiry, leading to the identification of Nichol Snipe, a local game-keeper, as the father. He and the maid are called to account by the kirk session and then duly appear before the congregation. While admitting he is the father, the gamekeeper seeks to make light of the proceedings by turning up wearing a wig on his head and another covering his face. He also wears two coats, one fastened traditionally and the other buttoned on back to front. Thinking initially that the accused has his back to him the minister orders him to turn around. The good Mr Balwhidder is momentarily confused but quickly recovers: 'Nichol, Nichol,' he declaims, 'if ye had been a' back, ye wouldna hae been here this day.' This, the novelist concludes, had such an effect on the congregation that the poor fellow suffered more derision than had he been rebuked in the manner prescribed by the session.

Today, we view such proceedings with a mixture of amusement and disbelief – perhaps even an element of relief that stoning wasn't one of the sanctions available for adultery! It is difficult to defend a system so reliant on gossip and tale-bearing, with its potential for settling scores and paying back slights, perceived or real. At the same time it is important to remember that the underlying rationale was to uphold a moral law reflecting the Christian ethic, as Calvin had sought to do in sixteenth-century Geneva. For the Reformers the marks of the true Church were the Word purely preached, the Sacraments rightly administered and discipline rightly exercised. Today social discipline is administered through a justice system where the arbiters are dispassionate and professional judges, a safeguard very far removed from the eighteenth-century church disciplinary procedures. One of the most appalling consequences of cases such as that narrated by John Galt was that it was not unknown for a young woman to kill her child at birth, rather than face the wrath of the session; only to find herself subsequently convicted on a charge of child murder and hanged. There are also records that testify to a practice whereby, in the event of paternity continuing unacknowledged, the women attending an unmarried mother were instructed to conduct an interrogation during childbirth itself. The phrase used by the Presbytery of Penpont was 'strictly questioned in her pangs by the women who shall be present'. Another inquisitorial option was the lacteal test, which involved the examination of a woman suspected of being the mother of a newborn child to see if there was milk in her breasts. No doubt those involved in such practices genuinely believed they were urging confession to save sinful young women and their lovers from the fires of hell. The fact remains, though, that as is still the case in many situations today, different standards applied depending on gender and class. The laird, too, was subject to church discipline but in his case it was more likely to involve a private admonition before the session, or even by the minister alone, combined with a handsome contribution to the poor fund.

Meantime, in other areas things were changing and even progressing. The strict rule that only psalms should be used in worship was challenged by the publication in 1745 of a collection of metrical paraphrases. These were based on a broader range of biblical texts, though another forty years were to elapse before they were generally accepted. One reason for the delay was that the prevailing Moderate party in the Church considered them 'too evangelical'. Today these paraphrases still provide a source of much-loved hymnody, including such favourites as 'O God of Bethel' and 'Father of peace and God of love'.

The final aspect of eighteenth-century congregational life to mention concerns Holy Communion. Calvin favoured a weekly celebration, Knox monthly (though he settled for quarterly), but by the eighteenth century, yearly or even every second or third year became the norm for many parishes. In part this reflected the time taken to examine and catechise parishioners, but there was also an economic consideration. The celebration involved not just Sunday but a long weekend from Thursday to Monday. Parishes took it in turns to host such gatherings, normally held in the summer months, with people travelling to whichever location had been designated. There the minister would be assisted by neighbouring colleagues and there would be a series of open-air preachings for the edification of the crowds. On the Sunday, a thousand or more might receive the Sacrament. The celebration continued through most of the day as relay after relay took their places at the long tables and a succession of 'fencing' sermons was preached. On the Monday, services of thanksgiving were held before the crowds dispersed.

The economic aspect arose from two points of view. First, there was a considerable burden of hospitality placed upon the host church and this became a factor in determining the frequency of celebration within the parish. Second, the diversion of so many people from work for so many days had implications for the largely agricultural economy. It should also be acknowledged that these gatherings facilitated activities other than those of an entirely spiritual nature, and these are well captured, characterised and caricatured in Burns' poem, 'The Holy Fair'. Preachers were branded as 'yuill (ale)' or 'kail-pot'. The former were dry and dreary and had the crowds heading for the beer tents; the latter were enthralling and compelling, so much so that people forgot about the soup that was left to simmer in the pot.

The Relief Church

Leaving the kail-pot and the business of the local congregation, it is time again to attend to the affairs of the Kirk at Assembly and Presbytery level and introduce another element in Scotland's mid-eighteenth-century ecclesiastical provision.

In 1749 controversy arose over the appointment of a minister to the parish of Inverkeithing. The patron's choice was a Mr Richardson but the people's choice was a Mr Adam. The Presbytery of Dunfermline backed the people and refused to induct Mr Richardson. A Commission of Assembly instructed the Presbytery to proceed but a year passed with no induction having taken place. A further instruction was issued and again ignored. The Presbytery maintained that ministerial promises of obedience to the courts of the Church were qualified by the phrase 'in the Lord' and so allowed conscientious objections to overrule obedience. Perhaps learning lessons from the Erskine case, the Assembly proceeded cautiously and came up with a compromise whereby Mr Richardson would be inducted by the Synod of Fife, a court higher than the Presbytery but lower than the Assembly. The thinking was that as the Synod covered a wider area, a quorum might more easily be found. However, a member of the Assembly, Dr William Robertson, dissented against this proposal. Robertson was making his mark as a leading member of the Moderate party, and in time would become Principal of Edinburgh University and a leading Scottish and European scholar. He argued that 'public regulation once enacted is absolute, and the right of private judgement is so far superseded that even those who disapprove of it are bound to obey'. This challenge was answered by the Evangelical party, who quoted from Chapter 20 of the Westminster Confession of Faith: 'God alone is Lord of the conscience and hath left it free from the doctrines and commandments of men which are in anything contrary to his Word'. These two positions neatly encompass the difference between the parties.

Eventually the matter came to the General Assembly in 1752, where the Lord High Commissioner, the Earl of Leven, directed the court as a judge might direct a jury. He uttered dire warnings against 'this growing evil' with its potential for 'anarchy and confusion'. The Lord Advocate, William Grant (former Procurator and Principal Clerk), even suggested 'enlightening the conscience of some ministers through their stipends'. This was a highly topical threat as a recent request for an augmentation of stipend had been refused by Parliament on the grounds that the Assembly dealt too leniently with presbyteries that refused to induct presentees. The Commission's proposal to have the Synod induct was rejected and a firm instruction issued to the Presbytery to proceed. Further, in a calculated turn of the screw, it was decided that for the purposes of this particular induction the quorum should be raised from the normal three to five. The reasoning was blatant. It was known that three members of the Presbytery were willing to induct Mr Richardson. The Assembly approved these arrangements and fixed the date for Thursday 21 May, just three days later.

The day arrived and the three members of the Presbytery turned up, ready, willing but, due to the ad hoc quorum, unable to induct. The General Assembly, still convened, summoned the Presbytery to appear the following day and six of its number dutifully did so. Once again there was a measure of improvisation that, from today's perspective, frankly, beggars belief. There was an obvious reluctance to depose six ministers, so the Assembly opted for a form of decimation and agreed to depose just one. A decision as to which one would be taken the following day. When the moment arrived the six were called, one by one. When it came to the turn of Thomas Gillespie, he read a document explaining his position and asked that it be entered into the records of the court. The Assembly refused and eventually the time came to choose the sacrificial lamb. A few votes were distributed among the other five, but fifty-two voted to depose Gillespie. Significantly, double that number abstained altogether.

Following the vote the Moderator, Dr Cumming, made a speech justifying the Assembly's dealing with the matter. Indeed, he congratulated the Assembly for doing what 'His Majesty's

Commissioner was pleased in his speech to recommend.' He then went on to stress the importance of upholding the authority of the Church and protecting the legal benefits of establishment, adding that the terms on which men were admitted to the ministry were well known. He concluded with an intriguing distinction. Anxious perhaps to acknowledge Gillespie's obvious decency, he observed: 'God forbid that those who cannot come up to those terms are not good men; but this may be said, that they are not good Presbyterians.'

Gillespie responded by acknowledging his sentence with 'real concern' and the 'awful impressions of the Divine conduct in it'. He also stated that he rejoiced 'that to me is given on behalf of Christ not only to believe in him, but to suffer for his sake'. He made no protest and without delay left his church and manse. It is said that when he returned home his wife's response to the news was: 'Weel, Thomas, if we maun (must) beg I'll carry the meal poke'. He preached in the open air until winter drew in and a barn was fitted up as a church for his use. A possible move would have been to join the Secession Church, though which branch? But he was not really of that mindset. He once remarked: 'I hold communion with all that visibly hold the Head and such only', and it is to this sentiment that today's Church of Scotland owes its policy of inviting members of any Christian denomination to share Holy Communion. For six years Gillespie continued his ministry until joined by Thomas Boston, minister at Oxnam, son of Thomas Boston of *Marrow* fame. Boston junior had departed the Kirk and formed an independent congregation at Jedburgh. Four years later a third congregation was formed at Colinsburgh in Fife and there, in October 1761, the Presbytery of Relief 'for Christians oppressed in their Church privileges' was constituted.

As a postscript to these proceedings it can be noted that, following Gillespie's deposition, the Presbytery complied and duly inducted Mr Richardson to the charge of Inverkeithing. The majority of the congregation accepted him and he had a good ministry. A note in the *Fasti* (a *Who's Who* of the ministry) states: 'Notwithstanding all the opposition and obloquy which he encountered he was an admirable parish minister, a good preacher and scholar of repute. During his incumbency not a few of those who had seceded returned to his ministry.' By contrast, the popular Mr Adams turned out to be a quarrelsome man who was never out of trouble. Those who left the Inverkeithing congregation in protest formed a Secession congregation and called Mr Adams to be their minister.

Disputed settlements continued to arise but, as just illustrated, disaffected church people were not short of alternatives. By 1766 it was estimated that between them the Secession and Relief churches had over a hundred places of worship. Meanwhile, for all its enforcement of the law of the land, the General Assembly continued with its annual protest making 'due application to the king and Parliament for redress of the grievance of patronage'. Not until 1784 did it resolve to discontinue what had long been a token gesture.

Further Divisions

When the Kirk adopted the Westminster Confession in 1647 it did so with a qualification concerning the role of the civil magistrate. In particular it asserted the right of the Church, on its own authority, to meet in General Assembly. The Assembly certainly believed that the State had a responsibility to assist and support the Church. At the same time the Kirk asserted its spiritual independence of the State; thus its fierce resistance to royal demands to rule the Church through bishops. In his *Institutes of Religion* Calvin expressed the matter thus: 'Civil government is designed, as long as we live in this world, to cherish and support the external worship of God, to preserve the pure doctrine of religion and to defend the constitution of the Church.'

As early as 1743 the Secession Church had published a 'Declaration and Defence of their principles concerning

Civil Government'. This clearly limited the magistrate's role to preserving good order 'without assuming any lordship over men's consciences, or making any encroachment upon the special privileges and business of the Church'. It is not difficult to see patronage as just such an encroachment and to understand why it was so fiercely resisted. There is, though, another aspect to the matter. In those days the Church was not funded by the offerings of the people, as it largely is today. Rather, responsibility for its maintenance, including the upkeep of churches, manses and parish schools, rested with the heritors (landowners). The offerings of the people were used for poor relief within the parish.

As the century progressed, debates on Church–State relations continued to be a source of tension within the Secession. They had left the Established Church to be free of state interference such as patronage, but they had not entirely abandoned the idea that Church and State have mutual obligations. As time passed, thinking began change and a new principle, known as 'voluntaryism', began to emerge. Essentially, this held that the Church should be entirely independent of the State. Of course, like any other voluntary association, the Church would be subject to the laws of the land; but in terms of its own organisation it should be financed by the voluntary givings of its members and generally oversee its own affairs.

As early as 1730 John Glas of Tealing was pioneering this novel approach. That year he left the Established Church to found his own 'Glassite' sect, which functioned as an independent congregation of Christian people. Glas queried the basic assumption that Scotland was a covenanted nation, like ancient Israel, with Church and State as complementary aspects of the one community. His reading of the Bible led him to the view that the Church was a spiritual community made up of people from all the nations, and that it should have no particular connection with any civil power. He expressed these opinions in a book entitled *King of Martyrs*, published in 1728, arguing that the Covenants were unwarranted by Scripture. For good measure he refused to subscribe to the Westminster Confession on the grounds that it laid duties upon the magistrate in the matter of religion. All this led to his deposition from the ministry, which in practical terms made little difference. His followers provided a small meeting house in Perth, where he practised a ministry based on the apostolic model described in the book of Acts. He celebrated Holy Communion every Sunday and his services were followed by a shared meal. This earned his fellowship the title of the 'Kail Kirk', as Scotch broth was the regular fare. Eventually the General Assembly revoked Glas' rather hasty deposition, on condition that he came back into line, as they saw it. This he would not do, continuing to attract new members and, indeed, congregations, which grew up around Scotland in places such as Dundee, Leslie, Cupar, Dunkeld and Galashiels, as well as the original Tealing and Perth congregations. In time Glas' son-in-law, Robert Sandeman, continued the ministry, attracting followers in England and North America, where the denomination (for such it became) was known as 'Sandemanians'. Compared with the feuding Seceders, the Glassite/Sandemanian approach may sound idyllic. However, a strict discipline was imposed. For example, it was unlawful to pray with someone who did not belong to the sect or to share a meal with a person who had been excommunicated. Unanimity of judgement was also part of the discipline, leaving dissenters with a choice between acquiescence and withdrawal. The last Sandemanian elder died in Edinburgh in 1999.

In 1791 the Anti-Burgher Synod received an Overture from its Glasgow Presbytery asking for clarification of passages in the Westminster Confession on the power of the civil magistrate. The matter came up again the following year when the Edinburgh Presbytery expressed unease over the requirement that ministers express their belief in 'the whole doctrine contained in the Confession of Faith'. As far back as 1747 the Synod, in a Declaratory Act, had recognised that circumstances change and that forms of expression used by one generation may not satisfactorily express the thinking of another. More specifically the Act had acknowledged that the 'degrees of light on these matters' and the particular circumstances of drafters of earlier documents gave an impression of conceding to civil rulers 'a lordship over the consciences of men', something that was inconsistent with the 'spirituality, freedom and independence of the Kingdom of Christ'. Over the years since the 1747 split in the Secession, a process of assessment and revision of texts had continued, welcomed by some, though not by others, who suspected a relaxation of the Church's attitude to the Covenants. Eventually the process led to a revised Testimony, which acknowledged 'that, as no human composure, however excellent and well expressed, can be supposed to contain a full and comprehensive view of divine truth; so, by this adherence, we are not precluded from embracing, upon due deliberation, any further light that may afterward arise from the Word of God, about any article of divine truth.'

This was a significant development that effectively distinguished between a 'statement' of faith and a 'definition' of faith. Humanly drafted statements are at best provisional and it is healthy that fresh eyes assess and revise these to ensure that they remain fit for purpose as generations rise and fall. The references to 'degrees of light' and 'further light' gave rise to the terms 'New Light' and 'Old Light' ('New Licht' and 'Auld Licht' in Scots) to distinguish between those who welcomed change and those who resisted it, but true to Seceder form, it was not long before difference of opinion led to separation. In 1806 a number withdrew from the Anti-Burgher Synod and, at Whitburn, constituted themselves the Constitutional Presbytery, more commonly referred to as the 'Auld Licht Anti-Burghers'. They took their stand on the original principles of the 1733 Secession and not on what they described as 'these late innovating acts'.

Meanwhile, a similar process had been conducted within the Burgher wing of the Secession Church, beginning when, in 1778, they published a 'Re-exhibition' of their original 1733 Testimony. However, it was not until 1795 that things came to a head with a plea for a relaxation of the formula to be signed by ministers on ordination and induction. Again the issues related to the role of the civil magistrate and the obligations of the National Covenant. Intense and fractious debates ensued until, in 1799, a small group protested and withdrew, declaring their 'simple and unqualified adherence' to their principles. In October of that year they constituted themselves the 'Associate Presbytery' and soon became known as the 'Auld Licht Burghers'. Those who remained were referred to as the 'New Licht Burghers'.

To complete this theme of divisions within the Kirk we have rather run on to the century's end and will shortly take a step back to consider other matters. However, the tale of schism is not quite told. Mention should be made of a further split within the Anti-Burgher wing of the Secession over the question of whether the minister, when celebrating Holy Communion, should lift up the bread and cup before the prayer of consecration. The arguments became quite heated, with 'Lifter' and 'Anti-Lifter' factions, not to mention a 'Lifter Presbytery'. Indeed, one controversialist even managed to produce a 216-page pamphlet on the subject. It would appear that, by the opening decade of the nineteenth century our shipwrecked Scot stranded on his desert island would have had to build several more churches to provide a full range of boycotting options.

The Enlightenment

In the preceding section the term 'new light' was applied to fresh thinking within the Secession churches on their relationship with the Covenants, particularly within the context of Church–State relations. This was a very narrow focus within a much broader process of Enlightenment that developed in eighteenth-century Scotland.

One of the leaders of this movement was William Robertson, whom we have already met on p. 112. Robertson had begun his ministry at Gladsmuir in 1744, moving in 1758 to Lady Yester's Chapel, Edinburgh. Three years later he became minister of Old Greyfriars, and the following year was elected Principal of Edinburgh University. Robertson's Moderate stance found expression in a number of ways. He had a strong commitment to intellectual and religious tolerance and, at the General Assembly of 1757, was instrumental in the defeat of a motion condemning the religiously sceptical philosopher David Hume. Later, at some cost to his reputation, he supported a move to repeal penal laws still in place against Roman Catholics. The attempt failed and Robertson's home was besieged by an angry mob, forcing the family to seek refuge in Edinburgh Castle. However, in the ongoing controversies over patronage and disputed presentations he was less tolerant. Robertson took the view that patronage was a good thing in that it ensured a supply of educated and cultured men for the ministry. To this day the Kirk sets a high value on an educated ministry. Of course, education has both breadth and depth. In the eighteenth century it was expected that ministers should be deeply versed in Scripture and Calvinist theology; but what about breadth of education? Novels were being written, plays were being performed in theatres and musical soirees were being held with dancing. The Revd Alexander Carlyle (nicknamed 'Jupiter' on account of his striking appearance) was possibly the first member of the clergy to take dancing lessons. He was also a theatregoer and very publicly attended a performance of a play entitled *Douglas* by John Home. For this the Presbytery of Dalkeith sought to rebuke him, but he declined to appear, maintaining that he had broken no laws of the Church. An appeal to the Synod on these grounds upheld his position. The Presbytery then appealed to the General Assembly, which again upheld Carlyle, thanks, in part, to the support of William Robertson. It was rumoured that Robertson had himself taken part in a rehearsal of the same play the previous year.

Late eighteenth-century Edinburgh was a place where

ministers such as Robertson and Carlyle met with other men of ideas. Robertson was a founder member of the Select Society, an Edinburgh debating society whose members included the artist Allan Ramsay, philosopher David Hume, economist Adam Smith and playwright John Home. Another gathering was the Oyster Club, founded by the geologist James Hutton, who had begun to develop theories on the age of planet Earth and the manner of its formation. The club met weekly in various taverns and its members, alongside Hutton, Robertson and Carlyle, included the chemist Joseph Black and the philosopher and historian Adam Ferguson (sometimes called the father of modern sociology). James Watt and Benjamin Franklin were visiting members. A revived Oyster Club meets monthly in today's Edinburgh. Inevitably, not all within the Kirk were comfortable with ministers engaging in such society and imbibing, along with their claret, radical theories about the age of the Earth. The received wisdom, based on the book of Genesis, was that God had created the world in six days and the date of Creation was considered to be the year 4004BC. This was arrived at by a calculation based on the number of generations between Adam and Jesus in the genealogy set out at the beginning of St Matthew's Gospel. Indeed, this date was printed at the top of the opening pages of Bibles that included a date reference to the events recorded in the text below. Today we might smile but the threat to such received wisdom from the theories of James Hutton was very real.

While the Enlightenment confirmed the existence of two parties within the Kirk, it should be noted that there were fine minds in both camps. There were differences, though, in style and approach. For example, when it came to preaching, Moderates often focused on practical morality, with illustrations drawn from poetry and popular literature, while Evangelicals preached on sin and grace, their sermons firmly based on Christian doctrine and amply illustrated from Scripture. Robertson's counterpart as leader of the Evangelicals was John

Erskine. On Robertson's appointment as University Principal, Erskine was appointed to Old Greyfriars, where he remained until his death in 1803. It is interesting and encouraging to note that opposing party leaders, with differing opinions politically, as well as in matters theological and ecclesiastical, could minister to the same congregation. An example of their political differences was Robertson's opposition to the demand by American colonists for independence, while Erskine supported them. They also disagreed on Roman Catholic emancipation, of which, as already noted, Robertson was in favour. Erskine was also an early advocate of foreign missions, something that received a cool response when raised in the General Assembly of 1796. Opponents argued that the Gospel could be preached only to civilised people, further pointing out that those who supported such a move tended also to be advocates of the abolition of slavery. It should be borne in mind that this was just seven years after the French Revolution, which many viewed as a disturbing example of where pressures for liberty could lead. When challenged to justify the case for foreign mission, Erskine famously responded by pointing to a Bible and saying: 'Rax (hand) me that buik (book)'. He died in 1803 but the cause he espoused was already being implemented though various missionary societies and would eventually be taken up by the Kirk in the new century.

The same tensions between Moderate and Evangelical are still apparent in today's Kirk, though the term 'liberal' has replaced 'moderate' and, of course, the issues are different. There are those today for whom the words of Scripture will have the final say on matters of controversy; and there are those who see new ideas and discoveries as shedding new light on our understanding of the Bible. Indeed, the phrase 'new light' goes back to the Pilgrim Fathers and the words of one of their leaders, John Robinson: 'for I am very confident the Lord hath more truth and light yet to break forth out of His Holy Word'. In Scotland the application of the term may have begun with reference to the

Confession and the Covenants, but by the nineteenth century it would have implications for the understanding of Scripture itself. The new century would also see a significant shift in the balance of power away from the Moderates and in favour of the Evangelicals.

THE NINETEENTH CENTURY

Initiatives Beyond the Kirk's Comfort Zone

As the nineteenth century opened, the Kirk was coming under new pressures from external Christian agencies anxious to engage with a world beyond the comfort zones of congregational life and General Assembly debates. Moves to engage in foreign missions may have been resisted in 1796, but this was to become one of the strong themes of the new century. As the British Empire expanded, many saw a real opportunity to obey Christ's command to take the Gospel to all nations. The last decade of the previous century had seen the establishment of the London Missionary Society and the Church Missionary Society, and in 1804 the British and Foreign Bible Society began its work of translating the Bible into different languages and dialects. The later decades of the last century had also witnessed the beginnings of a Sunday School movement through the work of people such as Robert Raikes of Gloucester. His 'ragged schools' sought to offer basic education to children from poor families who would otherwise have received none, and similar initiatives followed in Scotland. Yet these were bodies operating not only outside the Established Church, but often in the face of resistance from it. An illustration can be found in the work of two brothers, James and Robert Haldane, loyal Kirk members, yet frustrated by the Kirk's failure to engage effectively with people beyond its fold. So after dutifully attending church on Sunday mornings they would hold open-air evangelical rallies, attracting large crowds. This led to the creation of a Society for the Propagation of the Gospel at home, effectively an independent church movement, with a number of congregations that practised Baptism by immersion and held weekly communion services. In some ways they were following in the footsteps of Glas and Sandeman. They even had their own seminary. Such efforts, though, had been criticised by the General Assembly of 1799, which sent a pastoral letter to every parish criticising lay preaching, the Sunday School movement and the work of the London Missionary Society. At the same time there were those within the Kirk's Evangelical wing who recognised the need for such initiatives and took encouragement from them. Among those observing such developments would have been Thomas Chalmers.

Copyright © Peter Backhouse

Thomas Chalmers.

Chalmers was born at Anstruther in 1780. At the age of twelve he enrolled as a student at the University of St Andrews, where he studied and subsequently taught mathematics. In 1803 he was ordained and inducted as minister at nearby Kilmany, combining his ministry there with his teaching. In 1815 he moved to the Tron Church in Glasgow, by which time he had established a formidable reputation as a mathematician and as a preacher in the evangelical tradition. His Glasgow parish was huge, with a population of more than 10,000, many of whom had no church connection. Social conditions were appalling and in November 1817 Chalmers took his opportunity when invited to preach at a memorial sermon for Princess Charlotte of Wales, the popular daughter of the future King George IV, who had died in childbirth. In his sermon Chalmers drew attention to the dire social conditions among which he ministered, and urged a Christian response to the suffering of his parishioners.

Part of the problem was that the Kirk still operated a

parochial structure more suited to rural parishes and had no strategies for keeping up with the huge growth in city living. Between 1755 and 1831 the population of Lanarkshire had increased from 82,000 to 317,000, and of Renfrewshire from 26,000 to over 133,000. The sheer scale of growth in these areas around Glasgow can be seen when compared with the rise in the total Scottish population from 1.2 million to 2.3 million. In the spirit of Raikes and the Haldanes, Chalmers saw the addressing of pressing human need as a clear Christian obligation. In his opinion, Glasgow required at least twenty new churches, with ministers and elders working their parishes and raising both moral and educational standards. In this way the lives of individuals and the quality of communities would be greatly improved. As a result of his pressure the Town Council agreed to build one new church to serve a population of 10,000, and invited Chalmers to be its minister. He accepted and, in 1819, became minister of this new parish of St John's. His parishioners were working people and of 2,000 families, some 800 had no church connection. Relishing the challenge, Chalmers set to work with a will, organising the parish into twenty-five districts of sixty to a hundred families, with elders and visitors allocated to each. Two schools were established, providing lessons for some 700 pupils along with fifty Sabbath schools catering for around a thousand children. For Chalmers the two great social evils were irreligion and poverty. He further believed that these were connected, with the former being the cause of the latter. Many of his parishioners had been driven to the city by the unsustainability of living off the land, even with the prospect of kirk session poor relief coming to their aid. That had been the old model, but Chalmers still sought to apply it to St John's. His vision was to recreate a sense of caring community, where people looked out for one another and none were allowed to go hungry. At the same time his approach to poor relief placed great emphasis on family support. He did not advocate a national benefits system, fearing it would sap dignity and dilute the individual's resolve to get back on to his or her own feet. Essentially, for Chalmers poverty was a consequence of moral failure rather than what today we might view as political failings in the area of social policy. He did not rule out charitable support from the better off, but the main thing was the encouragement of a general moral and consequent material improvement in the condition of his parishioners.

From today's perspective this appears paternalist and amateurish, but at least it was a further expression of evangelical concern to reach beyond the congregational comfort zone and give expression to the Gospel not just in pulpit preaching and Assembly debate, but in the scenes of everyday life. What the Haldanes and others had been forced to do outside the Established Church was now taking place within it and under its direction. As the nineteenth century unfolded, others would challenge Chalmers' cause-and-effect link between immorality and poverty. For these later thinkers the elimination of poverty demanded political engagement to bring about improvement in areas such as economic policy, housing, wages, working conditions, education and health.

Foreign Missions

Arguably the first missionaries sent overseas by the Church of Scotland were the small group of ministers who accompanied the ill-fated Darien scheme. Essentially, their role was to serve as chaplains to the colonists but, in addition, they had been appointed by a Commission of Assembly in July 1699 to 'labour among the natives for their instruction and conversion, as you have access'. The senior minister was Alexander Shields, minister of the Second Charge at St Andrews, formerly a prominent Covenanter and the biographer of Richard Cameron. Arriving in Darien in November 1699 he made some expeditions inland but, struggling with the climate and frustrated by quarrels among the colonists, he moved to Jamaica, where he died of a fever in June 1700.

In terms of the century under consideration, we have seen how much of the pressure for foreign missions came from bodies outside the Church. One such was the London Missionary Society, and through this agency the twenty-one-year-old Robert Moffat from Ormiston, East Lothian, was sent to South Africa in 1816. His initial posting was to Namaqualand, an area of the Northern Cape bordering Namibia. After three years he returned to Cape Town, where his fiancée, Mary Smith, joined him from England. There they married and in 1820 made their way to Griquatown – a journey of some 800 miles – where the first of their ten children was born. She was named Mary, after her mother, and twenty-four years later she would marry David Livingstone. From Griquatown the Moffats travelled on to Kuruman, on the edge of the Kalahari Desert, where they established a missionary station. Before going to Africa, Moffat had worked as a gardener and farmer, experience that came in useful as he taught those with whom he shared the Gospel the techniques of soil irrigation. He also translated the entire Bible into the Setswana language and contributed accounts of his travels to the Royal Geographical Society. On visits back to Britain he spoke passionately in support of the missionary cause.

It was in 1824 that the General Assembly finally gave its support to foreign mission work and authorised collections in parish churches for this purpose. While this was a step of symbolic importance, the response to the appeal was less than overwhelming. Out of nine hundred parishes and fifty-four chapels of ease (church extension congregations), only fifty-nine parishes and sixteen chapels made a collection. But it was a start, and the first missionary to be commissioned by the Church of Scotland was Alexander Duff, ordained in 1829 for service in India. Missionary outreach was already underway in that country through the work of Donald Mitchell, who had arrived in Bombay in 1823 in the service of the Scottish Missionary Society. Others followed Mitchell and together they established schools for around 3,000 pupils. In 1829 they were joined by John Wilson, who founded Wilson College in 1832. Wilson's wife, Margaret, was a missionary in her own right, having undertaken training in Aberdeen. She took the initiative in establishing western-style education for girls in India. The Wilsons can also claim credit for successfully petitioning the General Assembly of 1832 with a view to bringing the work of the Scottish Missionary Society within the aegis of the Kirk. From 1862 to 1870 John Wilson served as Vice-Chancellor of the University of Bombay.

Duff's sphere of service was Calcutta, where he founded the Scottish Church College and helped establish the University of Calcutta. His medium of evangelism was education and he broke new ground by reaching those of higher castes. He also favoured the use of English in his teaching, astutely recognising that this approach would be attractive to people wanting to get on in the world. His policy worked – those attending his classes grew in number and his converts became people of some standing and influence. This was a complete change from earlier missionary efforts, which tended to focus on the lower castes and the poor. As with Wilson in Bombay, Duff played an important role in the development of the University of Calcutta. Another sphere of service was Madras, where John Anderson was appointed in 1836, to be joined three years later by Robert Johnston. Again the focus was on education with, through the efforts of Mrs Anderson, a particular focus on the education of girls, including those of higher castes.

Other well-known names associated with these endeavours, though in the second half of the century, include Mary Slessor and David Livingstone. Mary Slessor was born in Aberdeen in 1848, but grew up in Dundee, where the family had moved as her father sought work. Mary herself worked in the jute mills, and an enlightened policy (for its time) allowed her to spend half the day in the mill and half at school. Inspired by the story of David Livingstone she applied to the Foreign Mission Board of the United Presbyterian Church and, on 5 August 1876, arrived in West Africa, where she took up her role with the Calabar Mission in Nigeria. A particular challenge she faced was native attitudes to the birth of twins, which believed that one twin was fathered by an evil spirit. As there was no way of telling which one, both babies would be abandoned in the bush. Many such children were rescued and cared for by the Mission, with Slessor herself adopting a surviving twin, naming her Janie and bringing her on an extended visit back to Scotland.

David Livingstone was born in Blantyre in 1813 and died sixty years later in what is now Zambia. As recently as 2002 he was included by popular vote of readers of a national newspaper in a list of the one hundred greatest Britons. Both in his lifetime and the years following his death in 1873, he was a national hero, famed for his epic journeys of discovery across Africa. Reference should also be made to Mary Livingstone, daughter of Robert and Mary Moffat. She and Livingstone married in 1845. In 1847 they were posted to a new London Missionary Society station at Kolobeng in today's Botswana, where Mary taught and worked alongside her husband. Twice she crossed the Kalahari with him, while pregnant, the second time with three young children. However, Livingstone's African explorations led to the couple spending much time apart, with Mary and the children back in Scotland for schooling. She died of malaria in 1862 within three months of rejoining her husband in Africa. When Livingstone died in 1873 his remains were brought back for burial in Westminster Abbey; meanwhile, Mary's rest in a neglected grave on the banks of the Zambesi.

Today it is fashionable to view such missionary work as paternalist imperialism, furthering the cause of conquest and empire. As Desmond Tutu once put it: 'When the missionaries came to Africa they had the Bible and we had the land. They said, "Let us pray". We closed our eyes. When we opened our eyes we had the Bible and they had the land.' Inevitably, some of the tar from this particular brush landed on Livingstone, but one thing on which both fans and critics are agreed is his fierce opposition to the slave trade. His reputation in those countries where he served remains high and it is relevant to note that, against the background of colonial place names being replaced by African ones, Livingstone in Zambia and Livingstonia and Blantyre in Malawi stand out as notable exceptions.

Today's Kirk maintains strong and practical links with partner churches around the world, providing mission partners, welcoming international delegates to the General Assembly and ensuring that each year's programme of Moderatorial visits includes an overseas partner church.

Edward Irving and John McLeod Campbell

The interest in foreign mission was a clear expression of Christ's instruction to go and make disciples of all nations; but what about the many at home who remained unbaptised and unreceived into the life of the Church? Moreover, how did evangelism, whether at home or abroad, square with the doctrine of predestination, which held that salvation was for the elect and not for all?

The opinions of two young ministers brought such questions to the fore in heresy trials of the 1830s. John McLeod Campbell, minister at Rhu, was deposed by the General Assembly of 1831 for teaching the doctrine of universal atonement and pardon through the death of Christ. Essentially, the concept of atonement has to do with reconciliation, bringing together what is separate and making it 'at one'. Campbell argued that if the doctrine of predestination taught that the non-elect sinner was damned to all eternity, then the price of such sin was paid twice over – by Christ and the sinner. In the view of the General Assembly such opinions were contrary to Scripture and the Westminster Confession, and Campbell was deposed by a vote of 125 to 6. It can be noted that these numbers indicate that more than half of those entitled to vote failed to do so. The pronouncing of the Assembly's judgement was not without dark humour. The Clerk opined: 'These doctrines of Mr Campbell will remain and flourish long after the Church of Scotland has perished and been forgotten.' Of course, he meant it the other way round, but Campbell's friend and supporter, Thomas Erskine of Linlathen, is reported to have whispered: 'This he spake, not of himself, but being high priest, he prophesied', words originally used by St John to refer to Caiaphas' cynical comment that it was expedient that one man should die for the people.

Particularly significant in these proceedings was the Assembly's refusal to hear any Scriptural debate but to rely entirely on the Confession of Faith to settle the matter. In a stinging rebuke Robert Lee, minister at Greyfriars, observed that the courts of the Church had repudiated their Protestant character and followed the example of Rome, whose twin sources of authority were Scripture and Church tradition. McLeod Campbell himself adopted a similar line, referring to the plea of the first Reformers when they presented *The Scots Confession* to the Parliament of 1560. They had invited those who found anything amiss to draw attention to it and the matter would be referred to Scripture as ultimate authority. By the same token Campbell's parting challenge was to deplore a Church that says: 'I do not need to prove that what you teach is contrary to the Scriptures, it is quite enough that it is contrary to the Confession of Faith'. To this way of thinking his response was that a Church that uses such language no longer remembers its place as a Church. Following his deposition Campbell preached for a number of years at a small meeting house in Glasgow. Subsequently, his health failing, he retired to Rosneath. In 1855 he published his theological treatise entitled *The Nature of the Atonement*.

Edward Irving was a native of Annan and was ordained by that Presbytery. He had been an assistant to Thomas Chalmers at St John's Glasgow, where he was a popular and welcome visitor in the homes of the parish. From there, unable to find a patron willing to present him to a charge, he moved to a small

Scottish congregation in London, where his oratory attracted large crowds; so much so that a larger church was built for him in Regent Square. Thomas Chalmers preached at its opening. Gradually, however, Irving's theology began to stray beyond accepted bounds. He struggled with questions concerning the nature of Christ's humanity. Could he really be fully human *and* without sin? Irving also took an interest in Millennialism, the belief that Christ will rule over a thousand-year Golden Age on earth before the final judgement and the world to come. He also explored Pentecostalism through prophecy and speaking in tongues and was content to permit 'inspired' interruptions to his services. Unsurprisingly, this was unsettling for many worshippers and led eventually to his removal from the Regent Square pulpit. In 1831, the year of McLeod Campbell's trial and deposition, the General Assembly instructed the Presbytery of Annan to try him for heresy. A crowd of nearly 2,000 gathered to witness the proceedings and were treated to a two-hour justification of his views. However, his pleadings failed to convince the Presbytery, which voted unanimously for his deposition. Thereafter Irving continued to preach at meetings in London, and while he did not found the Catholic Apostolic Church, his name continues to be associated with that denomination to the extent that its adherents are sometimes referred to as 'Irvingites'. He died in 1834 at the age of forty-two and was buried in the crypt of Glasgow Cathedral. It is recorded that as the mourners departed there remained a number of young women, dressed in white, waiting for him to rise again.

The Ten Years' Conflict

This is the term given to the period from 1834 to 1843. The former year saw the Evangelical party gain a majority in the General Assembly under the leadership of Thomas Chalmers; the latter was the year of the Disruption. The decade also saw many cases of litigation as claims for spiritual freedom were challenged and aggrieved parties, unable to find satisfaction in the church courts, sought civil remedies.

The General Assembly of 1834 passed two major pieces of legislation. These became known as the Chapels Act and the Veto Act. Reference has already been made to the failure of the Kirk to adapt its parish system to the new Scotland of overcrowded city communities. What was called for was the building of churches to serve the needs of a growing population, particularly in towns and cities as people moved from the country. Many, indeed, were built and were known as 'Chapels of Ease', places that people found easier to attend than a parish church situated some distance away. However, at that time the parish church had a particular status, which included civil functions such as the calling of banns of marriage. Because of this the old parish churches were described as *quoad omnia*, the Latin tag signifying that the kirk session was responsible for 'all things'. By contrast, the new Chapels of Ease were designated as *quoad sacra*, making clear that their kirk sessions were responsible only for religious functions. There was a further crucial distinction, namely that parish ministers were entitled to membership of church courts; ministers of the new *quoad sacra* churches were not, and the purpose of the Chapels Act was to include them. From the Evangelical point of view this was a calculated move. Many of the ministers of the new chapels were of that party and would strengthen its influence over church policy.

The other piece of legislation was the Veto Act. This arose out of the long-running grievance over patronage. It should be borne in mind that in 1832, just two years before this significant General Assembly, Parliament had passed the Reform Act, which extended the franchise and set the country on a more democratic path. The Veto Act recognised the patron's right of presentation and required presbyteries to examine the nominee's credentials and suitability as before. However, it added a power of veto if a majority of male heads of families objected to the appointment. There was a sufficient majority within the

Assembly to pass both measures; but there was also opposition from the Moderate party, who feared the Veto Act was a step too far towards congregationalism and noted that past experience had shown that many successful ministries had been exercised by individuals initially frowned on by popular sentiment. It was not long before the new Assembly Acts were put to the test.

In October 1834 the Earl of Kinnoul presented Mr Robert Young to the parish of Auchterarder. After he preached in the vacancy only two parishioners signed the call, while 287 out of 330 male heads of families invoked the recently adopted Veto Act to block his appointment. The Presbytery, respecting that decision, took no further action. This, however, was far from the end of the matter, as Mr Young appealed to the Court of Session and a judgement in his favour was delivered in March 1838. This gave an opportunity for reflection before the General Assembly met in May, though not enough time for outrage to die down. The Assembly's response was to assert its claim to spiritual independence and refer the case to the House of Lords. A year later, on the eve of the 1839 Assembly, the Lords roundly dismissed the Kirk's appeal on the basis that patronage was a civil matter and the Church's role was simply to satisfy itself that a nominee was qualified in terms of 'life, literature and doctrine'. Any question of acceptability to the congregation was irrelevant. In short, the House of Lords ruled that in passing the Veto Act the General Assembly had exceeded its powers.

In response the Church held firm on the spiritual aspects of the case and refused to induct Mr Young. However, it did acknowledge the civil dimension by agreeing that Mr Young could occupy the manse and receive the stipend. At the same time a committee was appointed to negotiate with the government and seek a solution. A key difference between the Moderates and Evangelicals was that the former did not view ordination as an exclusively spiritual matter, since the parish minister also had a role within civil society. They viewed a congregational call as no more than 'a courteous convention'. The main thing was that the Presbytery should be satisfied as to the candidate's education and character. By contrast, for the Evangelicals, ordination was an entirely spiritual matter and the call an essential part of the process, as it had been since the Reformation. For the record, Mr Young was eventually inducted to Auchterarder, but not until after the Disruption. He went on to enjoy a fruitful ministry and his death in 1865 was much mourned by his parishioners.

Equivalent scenarios to Auchterarder were acted out around the country during the Ten Years' Conflict, though not always from the same perspective. It is worth mentioning another case concerning the parish of Marnoch in the Presbytery of Strathbogie. Such was the toing and froing there that the sequence of events became known as 'The Reel of Bogie'. The case is also of interest because it followed a rather different course from Auchterarder.

Following a vacancy in 1837 a Mr Edwards, who had been serving as assistant minister, was presented by the patron. However, only four people signed the call while 261 male heads of families exercised their right under the Veto Act to block it. Accordingly, the General Assembly of 1838 instructed the Presbytery to reject the presentee and the Presbytery complied. The patron accepted the situation and made a new presentation in the person of a Mr Henry.

However, Mr Edwards then sought an interdict from the civil courts to prevent Mr Henry's induction and raised a further action to compel the Presbytery to proceed with the various steps towards *his* induction to the charge. He was successful on both counts and, faced with this, the Presbytery decided, by a majority of seven to four, to obey the instruction of the civil court and defy the Assembly. As it happened, a Commission of Assembly was meeting a week later and, unsurprisingly, the matter was on the agenda. The Commission's response was to suspend the 'Strathbogie Seven' and order that Mr Edwards be not inducted. In addition the Commission appointed a number of Evangelical ministers to carry out the duties of those who had been suspended. To this the 'Seven' responded by obtaining interdicts preventing those so appointed from intruding into their parishes. Further civil proceedings by Mr Edwards resulted in a court order that the Presbytery was bound to induct him and, on a bleak and snowy day in January 1841 the suspended Seven constituted themselves a presbytery and inducted Mr Edwards. The church was well filled until the service began, at which point members of the congregation registered their protest and withdrew.

In May the General Assembly met and, on the motion of Thomas Chalmers, the Seven were deposed from the ministry and their parishes declared vacant. The induction of Mr Edwards was also declared null and void and the remaining members of the Presbytery were instructed to induct Mr Henry in his place. This they duly did. Meantime, the Court of Session responded to the depositions by suspending the Assembly's sentences of deposition and interdicting any steps to fill the parishes that had been declared vacant. They also found that the ministers who had inducted Mr Henry were in breach of interdict.

Cases such as Auchterarder and Strathbogie arose out of the Veto Act but there were also civil proceedings occasioned by the application of the Chapels Act. Following on the 1839 return of the Old Light Burghers to the Kirk, it was agreed that former Secession ministers should be full members of Presbytery in terms of the Chapels Act. One of the first congregations to take advantage of this was Stewarton, and arrangements were made to create a new *quoad sacra* parish within the bounds of the old *quoad omnia* parish and to admit the former Secession minister, James Clelland, to a seat in the Presbytery.

Objections to both steps were raised by the heritors, who argued that the power to create new parishes lay with the Court of Teinds. They appealed to the civil courts and were granted an interdict preventing the creation of the new parish and the inclusion of Mr Clelland within the membership of the Presbytery. The interdict was ignored and the Church proceeded with its desired policy. The case was then referred to the Court of Session, where it was considered by a bench of the whole Court comprising thirteen judges, who found for the heritors by a majority of eight to five.

Essentially, what was occurring was a clash of two jurisdictions. The Kirk claimed an independent spiritual authority with which the civil courts had no right to interfere. Certainly, the civil courts were content to acknowledge and allow the Church's exercise of its spiritual jurisdiction within its own sphere; but the pre-Disruption cases were not always clear-cut in this regard. For example, as previously noted, patronage was a civil right that landowners and others were legally entitled to exercise. Indeed, rights of patronage had a commercial value, being something that could be bought and sold. It is understandable that the Church should find this objectionable, but when it came to adjudicating between the civil and the spiritual, was the Church to be judge in its own cause? In effect, what the civil courts were insisting was that, if a dispute arose as to whether something lay entirely within the spiritual province of the Church or whether it also carried civil implications, it was for the civil courts to determine the question of jurisdiction. It was then for the parties to work through the consequences that flowed from that decision.

Against the background of cases, of which Auchterarder, Marnoch and Stewarton are three examples, the Assembly of 1842 adopted a 'Claim, Declaration and Protest anent the Encroachments of the Court of Session', usually referred to as 'The Claim of Right'. This made due acknowledgement of the 'absolute jurisdiction of the civil courts in relation to all the temporalities conferred by the State upon the Church'. The Claim then went on to protest over 'sentences of the Civil Courts in contravention of the Church's liberties', adding that rather than abandon those liberties the Church would 'relinquish the privileges of establishment'. Alongside this threat the Assembly sought political conversation with lawmakers with a view to resolving the matter. After all, the judges were only doing their job in applying the law. It was the law itself that needed to be changed so as to give expression to what the Church regarded as its entirely reasonable wishes.

However, things were not that simple. If the 1832 Act had given encouragement to those within the Church of a democratic mindset, it had equally raised concerns among those politicians who feared an unsettling of the established order and were no friend of democrats. There were also those strongly attached to patronage and others, from Dissenting backgrounds, who were distrustful of Established Churches such as the Church of Scotland. All-important personal relations were not good either, including a distinct lack of empathy and trust between Chalmers and senior Westminster politicians of the day. In short there was little willingness to compromise and in March 1843, after a long debate, the House of Commons rejected a proposal to set up a Parliamentary investigation into the state of affairs in Scotland. It should be noted that a majority of Scottish members voted for the proposal which, if carried, might well have delayed the Disruption and possibly averted it altogether.

With these civil court judgements and the rejection of an official inquiry into the Church's grievances, a deeply ominous scene was set for the 1843 General Assembly. As usual it met in May but that was the only usual thing about it. On 18 May the retiring Moderator, Dr David Welsh, preached at the opening service in St Giles' and, thereafter, took the chair as the Assembly convened for business at St Andrew's Church in George Street. However, following an opening prayer, Dr Welsh did not proceed to business in the normal way but read out a lengthy Protest. Then, after handing the Protest to the Clerk, he left the meeting, followed by Chalmers along with 121 ministers and 73 elders. They walked along George Street, turning right into Hanover Street, and continued through the crowds, some cheering, others hissing, down Dundas Street to the Tanfield Hall at Canonmills. There they constituted themselves the

General Assembly of the Free Church of Scotland. Thomas Chalmers was elected Moderator.

On 23 May an Act of Separation was signed and the final tally of departing ministers reached 474 out a total of 1,195. The sacrifice these men and their families were making was huge. They were leaving not only their churches but also their manses, all for an uncertain future, but on a matter for them of great principle. Schoolmasters who associated with the Free Church also had to leave their schools and schoolhouses, which were linked to the Established Church. Around a third of the Evangelical party remained within the Established Church with a view to influencing it from within. It is also important to mention a statement of Thomas Chalmers that would have great significance in the future: 'Though we quit the Establishment, we go out on the Establishment principle; we quit a vitiated Establishment but would rejoice in returning to a pure one. We are advocates for a national recognition of religion – and we

St Andrew's Church, known today as St Andrew's and St George's West.

are not voluntaries.' What he meant by this was that the Free Church still believed in the concept of a national Church whose role was, in effect, to represent the spiritual dimension of the State and, as such, to be supported by the State. In his view secular intrusion into the spiritual sphere had left the Kirk with no choice but to separate and assert its independence, but one day, he hoped, the breach would be healed and Church and State could again combine on a basis of mutual respect. The reference to 'voluntaries' also merits a word of explanation. This has nothing to do with volunteers. Rather, as noted in the previous chapter, it was the term used to describe the Secession and Relief Churches, which had long since gone their own ways and relied entirely on the voluntary giving of their members to fund their work. Inevitably, this would now be the position in which the new Free Church found itself, but Chalmers, at least, held to the hope that this would be a temporary measure pending an eventual healing of the breach.

The Establishment Question

In 1820 the New Light parties of the Burgher and Anti-Burgher wings of the Secession had come together to form a United Secession Church. In 1847, just four years after the Disruption, they were joined by the Relief Church, which had been formed in 1761. The name given to this new denomination was the United Presbyterian Church. As the Establishment fractured, the Seceders at last began to coalesce. One significant matter on which this new body differed from both the Church of Scotland and the Free Church was its principled opposition to the very concept of an Established Church. The United Presbyterians were proudly 'voluntaryist', the descendants of those who, having left the Establishment a century before, had become accustomed to paying their way.

Of course, having to pay one's way was now the position in which the new Free Church found itself. Those who had 'come out' in the Disruption had no church buildings in which to worship and their ministers had no manses in which to reside. The first task, therefore, was to raise funds for these purposes, and in time church buildings and manses were erected around the country. This was no mean achievement, and evidence of a deep commitment to the cause. Divinity colleges were also established in Edinburgh (New College), Glasgow (Trinity College) and Aberdeen (Christ's College). In time the Free Church also built its own Assembly Hall within New College, the Hall used by the Kirk today. In time such duplication of resources would create problems when a reunited twentieth-century Church found itself in possession of many more buildings than it needed. Today's all too familiar sight of former churches turned into warehouses, nightclubs, theatres and the like is a reminder of these former divisions. Many a small town remains in possession of three ecclesiastical buildings, representing the Auld Kirk, the Free Church and the United Presbyterian Church. Rivalries also played their part as a new Free Church building was erected cheek by jowl with the parish church, 'that the praise of the one might disturb the prayers of the other'. A similar spirit was expressed in a popular jibe: 'The Free Kirk, the wee kirk, the kirk without the steeple; the Auld Kirk, the cauld (cold) Kirk, the Kirk without the people'.

What became known as the 'Establishment question' did not go away. On the contrary it surfaced prominently in the 1870s, when pressure came from both the Free and United Presbyterian Churches for the disestablishment of the Church of Scotland. In 1870 the Anglican Church of Ireland was disestablished in face of pressure from the majority Roman Catholic Church, and similar moves were made in England by Liberals, Dissenters and Nonconformists, though without success. To this day the Church of England continues as the Established Church in that country.

The call for disestablishment was entirely consistent with the voluntaryist principles of the United Presbyterians but it was a clear change of policy by the Free Church. The move was strongly resisted by the Church of Scotland, one of the main defenders of the status quo being John Tulloch, Principal of St Mary's College, St Andrews. His arguments will carry less weight in today's multi-faith society but, essentially, his contention was that an Established Church was 'an institution ... embodying the great thought that religion is not merely a private but a public concern ... which deserves recognition, organisation and support'. Tulloch observed, somewhat waspishly, that the voluntaryist denominations, which he described as 'prosperous Dissent', tended to locate their churches in more affluent neighbourhoods. That may have made perfect economic sense, but it had the effect of leaving ministry in 'the poor and crowded localities' to the Established Church. It is precisely this argument that still underpins today's Kirk's commitment to a territorial ministry 'to the people in *every* parish in Scotland'.

At the end of the day the challenge to the Establishment principle did not succeed, though the issue would re-emerge in the reunion negotiations of the early twentieth century. It should also be noted that, finally, in 1874, Parliament passed an Act abolishing patronage, conceding that the nomination and appointment of ministers was entirely a matter for the Church. The effect of this was to place the Established Church in the same position as the Free and United Presbyterian Churches.

Renewal in Worship

We begin this section with a mildly amusing account from the year 1822. Reference has been made to the non-recitation of the Lord's Prayer in Presbyterian worship, though it was used in Episcopalian services. On 25 August 1822, King George IV, in the course of a visit to Edinburgh, worshipped in St Giles' at a service led by Dr David Lamont, Moderator of the General Assembly. On his way to St Giles' the Moderator fell in with his colleague, Dr Inglis, minister of Greyfriars Kirk. The two conversed and Dr Inglis remarked that, as Supreme Governor of the Church of England, the king would be accustomed to the congregation reciting the Lord's Prayer. This rather alarmed Dr Lamont, who wasn't at all sure that he had the prayer off by heart. The fortuitous encounter concluded with the two divines withdrawing to an adjacent close where, under Dr Inglis' supervision, the Moderator repeated the prayer, line by line, until he was word perfect.

In previous chapters we have outlined the form of worship in the sixteenth and eighteenth centuries. What was it like in the mid-nineteenth century?

The following account has come down of a service conducted in Berwick in 1850 by Dr John Cairns, a prominent United Presbyterian minister: 'As the town clock struck eleven the beadle climbed the pulpit steps with the Bible and Psalter under his arm and stood waiting at the foot of the stair while the minister entered, no sound breaking the silence save the creaking of his boots ... After the opening psalm came a prayer lasting fifteen or twenty minutes, a reading of Scripture, another psalm, a sermon lasting fifty minutes and delivered without notes, a second long prayer, another psalm and the blessing.'

We can calculate that the service would have lasted around two hours. With the exception of the singing of the psalms, the minister's voice would have been the only one heard and the psalms would have been unaccompanied, led by a precentor. Essentially, things had not changed all that much since the post-Reformation period. The stool of repentance had gone and church buildings were more cared for, but services continued to be lengthy and wordy affairs.

Pressure for change was coming from various sources, one of which was a rise in popularity of the Episcopal Church. People were attracted by a greater sense of solemnity, decorum and refinement in services that followed a more ordered liturgical pattern. In 1849 the Duke of Argyll published a booklet entitled *Presbytery Examined,* which called for improvements in Presbyterian worship. A similar plea came from Robert Lee, minister at Edinburgh's Greyfriars Kirk, who appealed for a greater sense of order and beauty in services. Pressure for change was also emerging as people travelled and became aware of other traditions; also an increasingly educated membership led to raised expectations in the quality of preaching and a diminishing acceptance of the principle that the occupier of the pulpit was six feet above contradiction. At the same time, inevitably, there were those who fiercely resisted any change.

Mention has been made of Robert Lee, supporter of John McLeod Campbell and minister of Greyfriars. Lee had a clear vision of what was required and a strong resolve to implement that vision. In 1845 Greyfriars had been badly damaged by a fire and Lee saw the rebuilding of the historic church as an opportunity to put his plan into effect. Stained-glass windows were introduced and a harmonium was installed to accompany the praise. A service book was prepared with congregational responses, people were invited to stand to sing (the tradition was to sit) and to kneel for prayer (the tradition was to stand).

Greyfriars Kirk.

These innovations were not received with universal appreciation and Lee was ordered by the Presbytery of Edinburgh to 'conform in future to the order and form of public worship ... presently practised in the Church'. Against this Lee appealed to the General Assembly, which mitigated the Presbytery's judgement to the extent of censuring him simply for reading prayers from a book. Lee's response was to bide his time, and after a pause of four years he replaced the harmonium with a pipe organ and re-introduced a printed liturgy for his services.

Clearly, Lee was ready to stand up for what he believed, but it took a toll on his health, and on the eve of the 1867 General Assembly he suffered a stroke. The hearing of a case brought against him, due to be heard by that Assembly, was postponed and then abandoned altogether on his death in March 1868. In a centenary memorial sermon preached in Greyfriars the then minister, Stuart Louden, commented: 'It now seems little to the credit of Lee's generation in the Scottish Church that cruel charges of "innovation" and even "popery" were levelled against this devout minister of the Gospel who helped his church to enter into more of her Catholic heritage.' Lee certainly had his opponents but when was that ever not the case for advocates of change? After his death the controversy subsided, but a Rubicon had been crossed and gradually the kind of changes for which he was pressing became acceptable and, indeed, welcomed by many.

Lee did live to contribute to the foundation of the Church Service Society in 1865. The inspiration for this came from an 1863 essay on Kirk worship by G. W. Sprott. Sprott argued for 'a self-constituted Society of the liturgical scholars who would ... draw up a book of prayers for public worship and forms of administration of the sacraments, as a guide to the clergy.' Inspired by this proposal, three individuals decided to meet and explore the idea. They were James Cameron Lees, minister at Eastwood (subsequently at Paisley Abbey, then St Giles'), George Campbell, also of Eastwood, and Robert

Storey of Rosneath (subsequently Professor of Church History at Glasgow University). Campbell's note of the meeting states: 'We three conspirators ... agreed to sound out the views of various like-minded ministers and to invite them to attend a meeting for that purpose.' The meeting duly took place and the Society was constituted. From these beginnings would emerge Assembly committees of 'Public Worship and Aids to Devotion', charged with the preparation of material for the ordering and enrichment of Church services.

Reference should also be made to the establishment of the Scottish Church Society in 1892 'to defend and advance Catholic doctrine as set forth in the Ancient Creeds and embodied in the Standards of the Church of Scotland'. This body grew out of the Church Service Society but its interests went beyond liturgy to a broader emphasis on the 'Catholicity' of the Church of Scotland, meaning the Kirk's place within the Universal Church, not just the Reformed and Protestant Church. In some respects both Societies were motivated by the same influences that had given rise to the English Oxford Movement earlier in the century. There churchmen such as Edward Bouverie Pusey and John Henry Newman had set out an 'Anglo-Catholic' agenda through the recovery of liturgical and devotional customs that had been abandoned at the time of the Reformation. In Scotland the founders of the Scottish Church Society, such as Thomas Leishman, William Milligan and James Cooper, adopted what became known as a 'Scoto-Catholic' approach, celebrating the place of the Reformed and Presbyterian Kirk within the 'One Holy, Catholic and Apostolic Church'.

With regard to congregational praise, we have seen how Scriptural paraphrases were introduced in the mid-eighteenth century. This allowed the people to sing verses based on a broader range of Scriptural texts than the metrical psalms, including passages from the New Testament. The first hymn book came in 1794 in the Relief Church. This was followed in 1851 by the United Presbyterian Church (of which the Relief was by then a part). Next was the Church of Scotland in 1870, with the *Scottish Hymnal*; then in 1873 the Free Church produced *Psalm Versions, Paraphrases and Hymns*, followed in 1882 by the *Free Church Hymn Book*. Finally, in 1898 the first edition of the *Church Hymnary* appeared, the product of co-operation among the Church of Scotland, the Free Church and the United Presbyterian Church – an encouraging omen of the reunions that by then lay not too far into the future.

More Heresy Trials

Reference has been made to the cases of John McLeod Campbell and Edward Irving, whose theological views were deemed unorthodox when judged against the standards of the Westminster Confession of Faith. The Confession continued to hold sway within all three sections of the divided Presbyterian family and it was, perhaps, inevitable that further controversy would arise. Two cases are of particular interest – one relating specifically to the Westminster Confession and the other to Scripture itself. The former concerned Fergus Ferguson, a minister of the United Presbyterian Church; the latter involved William Robertson Smith, Professor Old Testament at the Free Church College in Aberdeen.

Ferguson was a minister in Dalkeith, and in 1871 he found himself in trouble for declaring that the Confession was 'no exhibition of the Divine order of the universe, rather, an exhibition ... of the disorder of the human intellect'. Proceedings followed but a majority of his Presbytery accepted his plea for 'liberty to investigate ... everything in God's revelation, whether consistent or not with the so-called standards of the faith'. A minority, however, dissented and complained to the Synod (the United Presbyterian Church's highest court). There, again, Ferguson gave satisfaction, agreeing to sign a statement of the fundamentals of the faith drafted for the purpose. This brush with controversy did nothing to harm his career prospects and in 1876 he was called to a new United Presbyterian congregation at Queen's Park in Glasgow. When, a year later, he found himself called to account for his views by the Glasgow Presbytery, his new congregation's response was to increase his stipend and prepare to secede were their minister to be deposed.

Certainly, by the mid-1870s a move for what became known as 'Creed revision' was well underway. Ferguson was part of this, and in 1877 he argued his case in an Overture to the Glasgow Presbytery. This was no easy task. Some feared an undermining of the Church's core beliefs; others feared that a new Statement of Faith, if such could ever be agreed, might become more restrictive than the Westminster Confession. Out of these concerns there emerged a proposal to leave the Confession well alone, but to draft a Declaratory Act setting out the sense in which certain sections of the Confession might be understood. This approach was approved by a single vote. In a nice analogy a prominent minister, Dr John Cairns (whose service at Berwick was previously referred to) recalled a rough crossing from Hamburg to Newcastle, one of the problems being that the ship was too light in the water. 'We need, in these blasts, to have some solid cargo. It is the doctrine of grace … that alone will float us', he declared. Cairns was appointed joint-convener of the committee charged with steering the theological ship safely to harbour.

Meanwhile, back at Presbytery level, Ferguson found himself again facing a charge of heresy and the Presbytery appointed a committee to investigate the matter. Given that the Synod had already appointed Ferguson to serve on the committee investigating the wider questions he had raised, this was somewhat premature to say the least. Nevertheless, the libel proceeded amid much public interest – and it is fascinating to note the level of media attention given to such matters at the time. The *Glasgow Herald* revealed its sympathies in a leading article referring sarcastically to 'the ardour with which the prosecution advances to the slaughter of heresy'. In the event, ardour carried the day and Ferguson was duly convicted. An appeal to the Synod upheld the conviction but a measure of respect for Ferguson was reflected in a sentence of 'affectionate admonition', with Ferguson being allowed to remain in his post.

Meanwhile, Dr Cairns continued with his work, which resulted in a Declaratory Act being approved by the United Presbyterian Synod in 1879. To this day this remains a 'leading document' for the Church of Scotland in the area of doctrine. The Act made clear that the Westminster standards, 'being of human composition are necessarily imperfect'. On the issue of predestination the Act stated that this was 'held in harmony with the truth that God is not willing that any should perish'. With regard to the doctrine of salvation through Christ alone, the Act, clearly influenced by foreign missions and a world where millions had never heard of Christ, acknowledged that it is not for the Church to set limits on God's saving grace. With regard to Scripture, liberty of opinion was allowed 'on such points … not entering into the substance of the faith, as the interpretation of the "six days" in the Mosaic account of the creation'. In other words, the opening chapters of Genesis need not be interpreted literally.

Ferguson's challenge had been to the Confession of Faith. Simultaneously with the events just narrated, an equivalent process was making its way through the courts of the Free Church. This involved a brilliant biblical scholar, William Robertson Smith, and it concerned not the Confession but the Bible itself.

As a scholar, Robertson Smith argued that Scriptural texts should be studied in exactly the same way as any other ancient documents. In 1870, at the age of twenty-four, he had been appointed to the Chair of Old Testament in the Free Church College, Aberdeen. The seeds of trouble were sown in his inaugural lecture where, borrowing a phrase from Luther, he likened the Bible to 'the garment of Christ'. He continued: 'We do not lay hold on Christ by grasping his garment … but

Christ is wrapped in the historic record and it is only within this garment that faith can find him.' From this principle, he argued that 'we are to seek in the Bible, not a body of abstract religious truths, but the personal history of God's gracious dealings with men.' This thesis flew in the face of Calvinist understanding of Scripture, which the Confession declared to be 'infallible truth'.

In 1875 an article on the Bible by Smith appeared in the *Encyclopædia Britannica*. This reflected his study of the relatively new science of 'Biblical Criticism', in which he had taken an interest through contact with German scholars. For example, the article reported questioning of the apostolic authorship of parts of the New Testament. It also mentioned scholarly debate as to whether some New Testament texts contained genuine apostolic teaching or simply reflected the opinions of one particular school of thought within the early Church. The possibility of earlier evangelical writings being lost to history was also touched on. Such theories are generally accepted today. Smith was careful to the extent that his approach was that of a reporter passing on news, as distinct from arguing the truth of these opinions on his own account. However, even reporting such questioning of Holy Scripture created a great stir and led to mutterings as to Smith's suitability for the Aberdeen chair. An investigating committee was set up, which reported that while unable to find sufficient in the article to support a heresy trial, they felt it to be 'of a dangerous and unsettling tendency'. The committee also recommended that Smith's continuing tenure of his Chair should be considered. In response Smith asked that a proper process be put in place. This was duly done when the Free Church Assembly of 1877 resolved by 491 votes to 113 to proceed to a libel.

The prosecution fell to Smith's Presbytery of Aberdeen, which was faced with the difficult task of reducing the various accusations to a stated case. The procedure, it should be explained, involved two stages – relevancy and probation. The former involved determining whether the conduct complained of amounted to an offence, in this case heresy. Were that not established then the case would fall. However, if it were established, the next stage would be to prove that Smith had in fact committed the offence alleged. Eventually a charge running to 8,000 words was drawn up, to which Smith responded with a document running to 25,000 words. He did not exactly help his case by publishing this in the press before the trial. The trial itself was a great event in Aberdeen, and Smith took full opportunity of instructing the ministers and public generally on matters such as the authorship of Deuteronomy. The outcome was a failure to establish relevancy and so the only verdict available was acquittal. Against this decision a minority dissented and complained, and so the matter came back to the Assembly of 1878, the same year in which Ferguson faced his trial before the United Presbyterian Synod.

In Smith's case, despite a lengthy debate and a series of divisions, no final result was achieved; rather, the libel that had failed to meet the test of relevancy was amended and sent back to the Presbytery for further consideration. In the meantime, Smith was suspended from his teaching duties, though his salary was conserved. (Echoes here of the previous century's Simson case.) Further discussion took place in the 1879 Assembly, with a final decision anticipated the following year. Anticipation was certainly in the air, and on the day the 1880 Assembly was due to hear the case, queues began to form outside the Assembly Hall from early morning. Inside the Hall a compromise had been agreed between those who were anxious not to stifle academic inquiry altogether and those who wanted Smith convicted of heresy. The two parties to this deal were represented by Professor Robert Rainy, Principal of New College, and Sir Henry Moncrieffe, a prominent Evangelical minister and a former Principal Clerk of the Assembly. The deal was that Smith's appointment would be terminated by an administrative act rather than a formal censure. However, the plan faltered when a hardline faction, led by a Dr James Begg, demanded that the libel be proceeded with. Meantime, two further motions were brought forward by Smith supporters. One asked that the Assembly simply disassociate itself from Smith's ideas and admonish him; the other also sought admonition but went on to declare confidence in Smith. A noteworthy detail is that the mover of this last-mentioned motion was a Dr Reith, an octogenarian who had been present in the Assembly of 1831 when McLeod Campbell was condemned. Reith proudly declared that he had not voted against him. He also warned of the dangers of interfering with the search for truth and, referring to the original compromise proposal, pointed out that expediency served neither the Church's peace nor its credit.

Where there are more than two conflicting motions, Assembly procedure is for a vote to be taken among them all. If none achieves an overall majority, the one with fewest votes falls. Further votes are then taken among those remaining. Following such a series of votes it came down to a final vote between the proposal of Rainy and Moncrieffe for an administrative termination of Smith's appointment and the motion of Dr Reith to admonish but express confidence in Smith. A rather amusing account has come down of what then ensued. Having lost his motion to proceed with the case against Smith, Dr Begg was reluctant to support or commit his troops to supporting either of the two surviving ones. He decided therefore to sit tight until the last minute and see which motion attracted the greater number of voters into their respective lobbies. Observing that the Reith lobby was clear, while people were still waiting to go through the Rainy-Moncrieffe lobby, he relaxed and indicated that his men should abstain. When the result was declared, Reith's motion to admonish and express confidence in Smith received 299 votes while the Rainy-Moncrieffe proposal to remove Smith attracted 292. What Begg had failed to appreciate was that the younger men, who had supported Reith, passed through their lobby in sprightly fashion, clearing it more quickly than the older brigade, who had proceeded through their lobby at a statelier pace. The result was greeted with acclamation, and the Moderator was faced with the difficult task of admonishing Smith, who had just gained a significant popular victory.

It was, however, a short-lived victory. Within weeks further articles by Smith appeared in the *Encyclopædia Britannica*. Complaints were made and a Commission of Assembly was called to address these. Another investigating committee was set up, which reported back in critical terms. This time Smith was suspended from his teaching duties and, the following May, the Free Church General Assembly of 1881 ratified that decision by a majority of 423 votes to 245. Smith's status as a minister was not disturbed and, for fear of a possible civil action, his salary was conserved. This latter gesture Smith spurned. Almost immediately he was appointed joint editor of the *Encyclopædia Britannica* and, two years later, he became Professor of Arabic at Cambridge University.

Where did the Free Church go from here? The answer to that question is that it eventually followed the same route as the United Presbyterians by framing a Declaratory Act setting forth the nature of its relationship to the Westminster Confession. This duly appeared and was adopted by the General Assembly of 1892. It followed a similar line to the United Presbyterian Act of 1879, recognising liberty of opinion on 'such points in the Confession as do not enter into the substance of the Reformed Faith therein set forth' (though there was no attempt in either Act to define this 'substance'). It also distanced the Church from the doctrine of predestination, but on the subject of Scriptural inerrancy it was silent.

Unlike the 1879 United Presbyterian Act, the Free Church Act was not approved unanimously by its General Assembly. Two highland ministers and an elder dissented. They also seceded and, on 28 July 1893, at Inverness, constituted themselves the Free Presbyterian Church of Scotland. In doing so they took their stand on adherence 'to the Bible, in its entirety as the Word of God and to the Confession of Faith in all its doctrines as hitherto held by the Free Church'. Some 4,000 members associated themselves with this new denomination. In response the Free Church Assembly of 1894 passed a further Declaratory Act that made clear that the 1892 clarifications and modifications were 'not imposed upon any of the Church's office-bearers as part of the Standards of the Church'; rather, it was the case that those 'licensed or ordained in this Church, in answering the questions and subscribing the Formula, are entitled to do so in view of the said Declaratory Act'. In other words, liberty of opinion works both ways and individuals are free to adopt a rigorous or relaxed attitude to the Confession.

Like the United Presbyterian Act of 1879, these Free Church Declaratory Acts continue as 'leading documents' in point of doctrine within the constitution of today's Church of Scotland.

The Committee on Christian Life and Work

Alongside these controversies in the Free and United Presbyterian Churches, various new initiatives were being developed within the Church of Scotland. The principal agent of this was Archibald Charteris, along with his wife, Catherine. No heresy trials were involved.

Charteris was born at Wamphray in 1835, studied at Edinburgh University and exercised parish ministries in Galloway and Glasgow. In Glasgow he served the Park Church and during his time there he married Catherine Anderson, the elder daughter of Sir Alexander Anderson, advocate, entrepreneur and Lord Provost of Aberdeen. The couple met when Charteris travelled to Aberdeen to interview her father for a biography he was writing. As Lady Anderson's health was poor, it often fell to Catherine to act as hostess. In this role she established a reputation for conversation, wit, forthright manner and readiness to engage in debate with academics, churchmen, business and civic leaders.

The Park Church in Glasgow was one of the wealthiest in

*Dr Archibald Charteris
and his wife, Catherine.*

Used with permission of Church of Scotland Guild

the city but Catherine was no genteel lady of the manse. Rather, she involved herself in a mission set up by her husband in Port Dundas, an inner-city slum area. In many ways following the example of Thomas Chalmers at St John's, the couple developed a scheme of visitation and practical support for residents of the parish. Catherine's role was to establish a team of women visitors who organised mothers' meetings, Bible classes and provided various forms of practical encouragement and support, an approach that had the double benefit of helping the poor and challenging the rich.

In 1868 Charteris was appointed Professor of Biblical Criticism at Edinburgh University and held the chair until his retirement thirty years later. There is an interesting link with Robertson Smith in that Charteris was identified as the author of an anonymous review of Smith's *Encyclopædia Britannica* article on the Bible published in the *Edinburgh Evening Courant*. Charteris took a conservative approach to Biblical Criticism, and the review was not complimentary. Indeed, it is reckoned to have been one of the factors lying behind the move that led to Smith's trial.

However, what Charteris is particularly remembered for is his convenership for over twenty years of a new General Assembly Committee on Christian Life and Work. He was the driving force behind the setting up of the Committee in 1871, and under his leadership a raft of projects was initiated. These had a common aim of stimulating practical Christian witness at home and abroad. Three of these projects continue to this day: the Guild, the Diaconate and the magazine *Life and Work*.

The Woman's Guild was founded in 1887, and while Archibald Charteris is traditionally identified as founder, his wife deserves equal credit. Catherine served as first National President from 1895 to 1906, by which time Guild membership stood at 40,000. A colleague at the time observed that the Guild 'owes its very existence to her efforts'. From 1891 to 1901, Catherine Charteris edited a monthly *Woman's Guild Supplement* through which she challenged complacency, lack of female self-esteem and urged women to work together to overcome poverty and injustice. In her final column she wrote: 'There is much to be done in these dark times … and who can tell what an influence for good our great Guild may accomplish if sister grasp the hand of sister, stepping fearless through the night'.

Reference should also be made to another prominent Guildswoman of the period – Lady Victoria Campbell, eighth of twelve children born to the eighth Duke of Argyll and his first wife, Elizabeth. Lady Victoria's energy and determination were remarkable, not least in light of the fact that she contracted polio at the age of four, which left her severely disabled throughout her life. As if this weren't enough, at the age of fourteen she developed a life-threatening lung-abscess, but managed to recover two years later. Meantime, her mother suffered a stroke, and until the Duchess Elizabeth's death ten years later, Victoria devoted her life to her care. In 1881 the Duke remarried and at that point Victoria decided to make her home on the island of Tiree, which was part of the Argyll estate. This was a brave decision as there was considerable crofter dissatisfaction towards her father. However, she was able to overcome this by her commitment to the islanders and her efforts in forming mothers' clubs and Woman's Guild branches, establishing milk and soup kitchens, securing nurses for the island communities and even organising a school for wood carving for the young men of Tiree. She also founded Guild branches at St Columba's and Crown Court Churches in London and was instrumental in the creation of a Guild branch at St Giles' in Edinburgh in 1904.

Another Charteris initiative was the institution of the Diaconate as an order of ministry within the Church. A particular benefit of this was that it opened a sphere of ministry to women at a time when their admission to the ministry lay nearly a century into the future. The first deaconess to be ordained was Lady Grisell Baillie in a service on 9 December 1888 at Bowden Kirk, where she and her brother Robert ran the Sunday School for nearly fifty years. Lady Grisell was also a great supporter of the Young Women's Christian Association and of the Church's foreign missions. She was the principal speaker at the first Woman's Guild national conference held in Edinburgh in November 1891, where she gave an impassioned address delivered, in the words of a contemporary report, 'in ringing tones as of a silver trumpet'.

The diaconal scheme included the establishment of the St Ninian's Mission on Edinburgh's Pleasance, where deaconesses could be trained for service both at home and abroad. Opened in 1889, the Mission provided practical outreach and support among the overcrowded tenements of the Pleasance and Cowgate. In 1894 a hospital opened next door, named the Lady Grisell Baillie Memorial Hospital, later called the Deaconess Hospital. Deaconesses undertook part of their training there and those who wished to become nurses could continue for a further three years at the Nurses' Training School. Like the Guild, the Diaconate today is open to both women and men, and deacons take their place, alongside ministers and elders, in the courts of the Church.

The third continuing legacy of Charteris and his Committee is the magazine, *Life and Work*, first published in 1879 and still providing a valuable channel of communication and information for church members. In its early years the magazine ran various supplements, including the Guild supplement and the *Young Men's Supplement*. The only one still going is the *Gaelic Supplement*, which was begun in 1880 and is read by Gaels all over the world.

Charteris was appointed Moderator of the General Assembly of 1892.

In the spirit of the Committee on Church Life and Work, though not associated with Charteris, the late nineteenth century saw the creation of two significant Church related youth organisations – the Boys' Brigade, founded by William Smith in 1883, and the Girls' Guildry, founded by William Francis Sommerville in 1900 – both in Glasgow. In 1964 the Girls Guildry amalgamated with the Girls' Brigade of Ireland and the Girls' Life Brigade of England under the name of the Girls' Brigade.

Partial Reunion

The abolition of patronage in 1874 led many within the Church of Scotland to think this might now open the door to union with the Free Church. However, the issue of Establishment remained; moreover, the Kirk now had the double benefit of being free to choose its own ministers *and* to have these ministers paid out of the historic revenues from the heritors to which the Church remained entitled. This hardly looked like a level playing field. So in 1875 the Free Church Assembly declared 'that the existing connection between Church and State ... ought to be brought to an end in the interests alike of national religion and Scottish Protestantism'. The voting was not unanimous, with 397 in favour and 84 against. The minority was led by James Begg, who later would so oppose Robertson Smith. He and his supporters still clung to Chalmers' vision of a Church that enjoyed all the benefits of Establishment and endowment, while also free to regulate its life in matters spiritual. However, the Free Church policy shift on the Establishment question was significant, for it meant that Church now shared the voluntaryist stance held from the beginning by the United Presbyterians. Surely, then, the obvious next step was for these two bodies to unite. Talks got underway and the Church of Scotland was included, partly to observe but also because there were those who still thought a triple union would be possible. However, there was strong resistance from the United Presbyterians to anything that might be described as a 'State Church'.

In 1893 the United Presbyterian Church Moderator spoke at a ceremony marking the fiftieth anniversary of the Disruption and stated that, from his Church's perspective, there was no obstacle to a union with the Free Church. The following year several Overtures were presented to the Free Church Assembly, all in favour of such a union. At the same time there were those who still pressed for talks to include the Church of Scotland. Rather ominously, a prominent Free Church lawyer, Taylor Innes, wrote to Principal Rainy, 'leader' of the Free Church, expressing concern about risk to property rights should the two-way union go ahead. Rainy replied breezily to the effect that people should not be deterred from following their convictions by legal opinion. Gradually, those who sought a wider three-church union accepted the view that this should be approached in stages.

In 1897 it was the turn of the United Presbyterians to cele-brate their Jubilee, and Free Church representatives reciprocated the friendly comments of four years earlier. In the Free Church Assembly of 1898 an indicative vote in favour of union was carried by 486 votes to 41. The forty-one held to the position that the Free Church was preparing to abandon distinctive points of principle, since the concept of an Established Church was a fundamental tenet of its constitution. The matter returned to the Assembly of 1900 for a final decision. To those still uneasy, Rainy adhered to his earlier line of not being intimidated into abandoning convictions by legal opinion. When the definitive vote was taken, the motion to unite with the United Presbyterian Church was carried by 586 votes in favour with only 29 against. The United Presbyterian Assembly also voted in favour that year. Their vote was unanimous. They had also consulted kirk sessions, where they had found overwhelming support.

This, however, was far from the end of the story. The date fixed for the union was 30 October 1900. The plan was that on the 29th both bodies would meet separately to finalise arrangements. Then, on the day itself, each would set off in procession, with the processions converging as they approached the Waverley Market, the only venue in Edinburgh large enough to accommodate such a gathering. There the new United Free Church would be constituted. On the 29th the business proceeded smoothly with the United Presbyterians. However, this was not the case in the Free Church Assembly. Over the summer a Free Church Defence Committee had been established and had taken 'eminent legal opinion', which advised them of their title 'to the Church's name, privileges and property'. They also presented a petition signed by 500 elders complaining that, unlike the United Presbyterian Church, the Free Church had not sought the views of kirk sessions. Against this minority view had to be set the overwhelming desire among members of both denominations for union. A final vote in favour of proceeding was carried by a resounding majority of 643 to 27.

The minority still refused to be bound by the majority, for they considered profound principles were at stake. The Revd J. Kennedy Cameron protested that those who had voted for union had elected to withdraw from the Free Church and that, once they had departed, he and his supporters would continue with the business of the Assembly. Effectively, they were saying to the

643: 'You go and join the new United Free Church if you wish; but we are going nowhere and the Free Church will continue.' They might well have added: 'and we'll see you in court!'

Six weeks later a Court of Session citation was served on the trustees of the former Free Church and the members of the Assembly who had joined the United Free Church. By this means nine ministers and eleven elders who had opposed the union asserted their claim to the entire property of the Free Church. The United Free Church responded with a counter-claim in which they pointed to an 1844 Trust Deed in which the Free Church had declared their church buildings to be held for 'a congregation of the said body of Christians called the Free Church of Scotland, or of any united body or bodies of Christians as the said Free Church of Scotland may, at any time hereafter, associate themselves ... under whatever designation they may assume'. The stage was thus set for the Free Church case that would take four years to pass through the law courts of the land.

THE TWENTIETH AND TWENTY-FIRST CENTURIES

The Free Church Case and its Aftermath

The Union of the Free and United Presbyterian Churches was not a smooth process. The minority resistance was on two grounds: first, that Chalmers' 1843 commitment to the Establishment principle had expressed a fundamental tenet of the Free Church and second, that the 1892 Declaratory Act had qualified the Church's adherence to the Westminster Confession of Faith. In response it was argued that, while an eventual return to a 'pure' Establishment had been an aspiration in 1843, it was not a fundamental belief. With regard to the second point it was contended that the purpose of the Declaratory Act was to address difficulties that many felt in subscribing the Confession, something that was perfectly legitimate for the Church to do. A legal judgement of 1901 accepted this defence, whereupon the minority appealed, though without success. The matter was then further appealed to the House of Lords, where their Lordships' approach was to view the Free Church as a Trust that had received funds on the basis of holding certain beliefs and principles. The key question then was whether, having modified these beliefs and principles in the manner complained of, it retained the right to hold these assets. By five votes to two the Lords decided it did not and, in 1904, found in favour of the dissenters.

The effect of this judgement was to throw ecclesiastical Scotland into turmoil. The entire property of the Free Church – hundreds of churches, halls and manses, along with three divinity colleges – was declared to belong to the tiny remnant that had rejected the union. Clearly, the situation was untenable and efforts were made to achieve a sensible sharing of the properties. However, at the end of the day the only practical way forward was for a Parliamentary Commission to deliver an equitable sharing. This was legislated for under the Churches (Scotland) Act, 1905, though the task would take ten years to complete. There was, however, a silver lining. Popular outrage at the Lords' judgement confirmed the commitment of those who had entered the union and drew a clear line between them and those who had chosen the path of separation.

While not directly affected, the Church of Scotland took the opportunity of Parliamentary involvement to review its own relationship with the Westminster Confession. As an Established Church the Kirk was not free to modify its terms of adherence as the non-Established Churches had done. It therefore obtained a provision in the Churches (Scotland) Act authorising it to amend the formula of subscription used by ministers and elders. In future they would acknowledge the Confession to be 'the Confession of this Church' and affirm their belief 'in the fundamental doctrines of the Christian Faith contained therein'. This form of words recognised a distinction between the faith of the Church and the particular beliefs of the individual, and allowed for a measure of liberty of opinion on matters that did not enter into the substance of the faith. In any dispute as to whether a particular belief was 'of the substance of the faith' it would be for the Church to determine the matter. Clues as to what might not lie within the substance of the faith had been given in the Declaratory Acts of the late nineteenth century: for example, the interpretation of the seven days in the creation narrative at the beginning of Genesis. It would therefore be an entirely credible position for a minister or elder not to take that account literally.

Further Church Union

Once things began to settle after the fallout from the Free Church case it was only natural that union between the Church of Scotland and the United Free Church should be explored. The ministers and members of both had much in common: for example, the same college curriculum, Presbyterian government, similar styles of worship and shared hymnody and psalmody. So it was that in 1907 the General Assembly of the Church of Scotland received a number of Overtures from presbyteries calling for joint conversations 'on the present unsatisfactory religious condition of Scotland'. A committee was appointed under the convenership of Dr Norman Macleod and by 1909 a joint committee had begun work on exploring 'the main causes which keep the Churches apart'. Norman Macleod and Lord Balfour of Burleigh led for the Kirk, with John White as Secretary. For the United Free Church, Archibald Henderson and George Robertson were appointed co-conveners, with Professor Alexander Martin as Secretary.

It was readily acknowledged that the two main issues for discussion were spiritual independence and the national recognition of religion. Significant differences existed between the two denominations on both counts. The United Free Church had been badly bruised by the legal proceedings that had concluded that it was not as free as its name might suggest. Meanwhile, on the Church of Scotland side it could not be assumed that everyone acknowledged spiritual independence as an unqualified benefit. Reference was made in the previous chapter to the Scottish Church Society, founded in 1892, to assert the Kirk's Catholic pedigree alongside its Reformed credentials. Two prominent members of the Society, James Cooper and A. W. Wotherspoon, were on the Kirk's negotiating team and they were anxious that the Church should adhere to the historic faith of the Universal Church. This, they argued, was expressed in ancient texts such as the Apostles' and Nicene

Creeds, but also safeguarded in the Westminster Confession. In their view, far from undermining the Church's liberty the statutory entrenchment of the Confession safeguarded the Church's identity within the one, Holy, Catholic and Apostolic Church. It followed, therefore, that for men like Cooper and Wotherspoon the notion of the Church having the freedom to change its Creed by majority vote of General Assemblies was not something to be welcomed. On the other side of the argument a prominent theologian on the United Free Church team, Professor James Denney, was wary of such an approach, regarding it as too rigid. For him a simple statement such as; 'I believe in God through Jesus Christ, His only Son our Saviour' was sufficient. Denney also argued for the freedom of individual believers to think out their own personal faith within the context of a Church that had the freedom to vary the forms in which its beliefs were expressed.

There were those on the Church of Scotland side who felt that Cooper and Wotherspoon were rather setting themselves up as sole guardians of the faith and resented their implication that what was being envisaged was a creedless Church. At the same time there was support for the general principle they were defending. This led, eventually, to the idea of a 'basal creed', namely a statement of fundamental doctrines setting out the Church's core beliefs, which would form an essential part of its constitution. However, from the United Free Church side there was some unease as to whether 'essential' meant 'unalterable'. By 1911 a measure of agreement was reached, with reports to both General Assemblies. These affirmed the Word of God in Scripture to be the Church's supreme standard of faith and practice. The reports also acknowledged the Church's right to frame, adopt and adjust subordinate standards from time to time, provided these were in conformity with the Word of God. Provision was also made for the liberty of individual conscience. The joint report was well received by the United Free Church Assembly; less so by the Church of Scotland, where there was a continuing concern to draw up a statement of fundamental doctrines that a reunited Church could present to the State as a summary of its core beliefs.

This brings us to the other crucial point alongside spiritual independence, namely the relationship of a reunited Kirk to the State. Prior to the 1900 union the Free Church had effectively abandoned the idea of an Established Church and, of course, the United Presbyterians had never supported it; meantime, the Church of Scotland continued on precisely that basis. Could a way be found that preserved the principle of a national Church while avoiding any suggestion of State oversight and control?

On this point those charged with conducting the negotiations found it helpful to look back to the period of the Reformation. In 1567 the Scottish Parliament had 'declared and granted' jurisdiction to the Reformed Kirk, and there were those within the United Free Church, such as Taylor Innes, a prominent lay member and lawyer, who argued that this meant that the Church was the creature of the State and thus reliant on benefits and privileges that could at any time be withdrawn. In response to this, Lord Sands, Procurator (senior legal adviser) of the Church of Scotland, put forward a persuasive counter-argument. He opined that between 1560 and 1567 the source of ecclesiastical jurisdiction in Scotland had been uncertain as both Reformed and Catholic structures existed side by side. However, following the abdication of Mary Queen of Scots and the coming to the throne of her infant son as James VI, Parliament, at the request of the General Assembly, had passed new legislation establishing the Reformed Church. The terms of the Assembly's petition to Parliament had asked 'that to this our Kirk be grantit … freedom, privilege, jurisdiction and authority'. Referring to this, Lord Sands first noted that the word 'grant' had been used by the Church itself. More significantly he pointed out that the term was generally used in legal documents not to signify 'giving' but 'acknowledging' or 'recognising'. It followed, therefore, that what had occurred in 1567 was not a delegation of authority by Parliament to the Reformed Church but, rather, Parliament's recognition of an authority already possessed by the Church.

In 1913 the Church of Scotland's General Assembly instructed its Union Committee to draft a constitution for a united Church, and this led to the preparation of *Articles Declaratory of the Church of Scotland in Matters Spiritual*. The first Article is, in effect, a statement of fundamental beliefs, though not an exhaustive one. It concludes with a reference to the Scriptures as 'the supreme rule of faith and life and avows the fundamental doctrines of the Catholic faith founded thereupon'. The choice of the word 'Catholic' reflects a victory for Cooper and Wotherspoon. In total nine Articles were prepared, including the right of the Church to interpret and, indeed, modify or add to them. However, any such change had to be consistent with the provisions of the first article, it being made clear that adherence to this 'as interpreted by the Church is essential to its continuity and corporate life'. A very high bar was also set for amending the Articles, namely the agreement of three successive General Assemblies with the approval of at least two-thirds of presbyteries in the two intervening years. Further, any amendment had to be consistent with the first Article. It should also be noted that the wording of the third Article very deliberately speaks of *a* national Church, not *the* national Church. Note also the lower-case 'n'. This role is further explained in terms of service rather than prestige, namely 'a distinctive call and duty to bring the ordinances of religion to the people in every parish of Scotland through a territorial ministry'.

With reference to the procedure for amending the Articles, only one amendment has been made since their adoption. This was in 1992 and involved the abolition of Synods, the court between the Presbytery and General Assembly. Increasingly, Synod meetings were poorly attended and, in practice, appeals taken from Presbytery to Synod were regularly further appealed to the General Assembly.

Inevitably, the First World War interrupted the negotiations; but the fact that members and ministers of both Churches were deeply affected by that catastrophe served only to underline the need for a final push to achieve union. The Articles Declaratory were approved by the General Assemblies of both Churches in 1919, and this opened the way for an approach to Parliament and the preparation of the Church of Scotland Act, 1921. This recognised the Church's spiritual independence in matters of worship, government, doctrine and discipline while, at the same time, safeguarding the jurisdiction of the civil courts in matters of a civil nature. The Act also made clear that nothing in it 'shall prejudice the recognition of any other Church in Scotland as a Christian Church protected by law in the exercise of its spiritual functions'. A prominent English churchman, Lord Hugh Cecil, summed up the achievement of the Act as 'harmonising with a definiteness and completeness for which I think no parallel in Christian history is to be found, the national recognition of Religion with the spiritual freedom of the Church'.

This notable achievement, however, was not the end the road. A major difference between the two Churches lay in the fact that many Church of Scotland ministers received at least part of their stipends from the teinds, the revenues to which the Church was entitled from the owners of land. This was something that went back to the eleventh century, when landowners consecrated one-tenth of the produce of their lands to sustain a Christian ministry for the people on their estates. A 1567 Act of Council described these tenths or teinds as the 'proper Patrimonie' of the Kirk. Churches, manses and glebes (land that was available for the minister to work and from which he might derive some income) were also part of the ancient patrimony of the Established Church. These assets were provided by landowners (known as heritors) as part of their legal responsibilities. None of these benefits accrued to the United Free Church which was entirely self-financing. Both parties agreed that these assets should now be brought under church control and continue to be used for their original purposes. This, though, was not a matter for the Church alone to determine. The heritors also had an interest, and a Government Commission was set up to address the matter. This resulted in a further Act of Parliament, known as the Church of Scotland (Properties and Endowments) Act, 1925. Under this legislation a process of standardising teind stipends began. Meantime, the various properties formerly vested in the heritors were transferred to a new statutory corporation, established in 1921 and known as 'The Church of Scotland General Trustees'. By this means these assets became the absolute property of the Church. At the same time heritors would make a fixed payment to the General Trustees in respect of endowment funds. This could be paid over a number of years, and would release the heritors from further financial obligations in respect of stipend or maintenance of the transferred properties. These standardisations of stipend and valuations of property and endowments were not inflation proof. When the present writer was ordained and inducted to his first charge in 1971, the annual stipend was £1,000, of which £350 (35%) was met by an endowment. In the 1920s that sum would have met the entire stipend. By the 2020s it will cover around 1%.

Further work continued on a detailed Basis and Plan of Union, which was approved by both General Assemblies in 1929. As in 1900, it was not to be a total reunion. A small minority within the United Free Church remained concerned about what they perceived to be inadequate guarantees on spiritual independence. Accordingly, they chose to continue as a separate denomination. Mercifully, there was no repeat of the rancour and litigation of 1900 to 1904. On 2 October the union was formally constituted in the presence of the Duke and Duchess of York (future George VI and Queen Elizabeth), the Duke acting as Lord High Commissioner and representing his father, King George V. Dr John White, minister at the Barony Church, Glasgow and Secretary to the Church of Scotland's

Union Committee, was elected Moderator, a role that he had filled four years previously in the pre-union Church of Scotland. The combined communicant membership of the reunited Church was a little under 1.3 million, comprising some 760,000 from the Church of Scotland and 540,000 from the United Free Church.

The Role of Women in the Church

The limited reference to women in previous chapters is quite striking, given that women have played a vital role in congregational and parish life, often as generous donors of funding and furnishings. Some, such as Catherine Charteris, Victoria Campbell and Grisell Baillie were able to play more prominent roles, but even they could never have been considered for ordination and admission to a role in the government of the Church. That said, one interesting exception to complete male control is worthy of note. Following the first Secession of 1733 the Seceders prepared a Testimony that declared that ministers and office-bearers should be chosen by the call and consent of the majority of members in full communion. Noting that women came into this category, some argued that women were thus entitled to vote. In response it was countered that the Testimony had been carelessly drafted and that it meant nothing of the sort. However, when the Secession split in 1747 over the Burgess Oath, the more progressive Burgher Church did allow women to vote, though the Anti-Burghers did not. In 1820, when the United Secession Church was formed by a union of the New Light wings of both Seceder factions, it was decided that women in full communion could vote equally with the men. The same entitlement was given by the Free Church following the Disruption. It is also worth noting that, while rare, there were some women who exercised a right of patronage, giving them a powerful voice in the appointment of a minister.

Moving forward again to the twentieth century and the re-united Church of Scotland, it was not long before the rights of women became a live issue. In 1931 a petition was presented to the General Assembly by the Marchioness of Aberdeen, a formidable advocate for women. When Lady Aberdeen argued her the case before the Assembly she was President of the International Council of Women and a recently appointed Dame Grand Cross of the Order of the British Empire. Her petition, bearing 338 signatures, called for women to be ordained to the ministry and eldership and to have access to all other positions within the Kirk. 'The continued exclusion of women from these offices', she maintained, 'is contrary to the mind and teaching of Christ and limits the operation of the Spirit of God.'

The petition was referred to the quaintly named Committee on the Place of Women in the Church. The following year two further, though less forceful petitions were presented. One was from the Woman's Guild asking that a number of women be granted corresponding membership of the Assembly, with a right to speak but not to vote. The other proposed that, rather than considering eldership and ministry, the Church should seek to develop existing opportunities for women. These petitions were also remitted to the Committee, which reported back in 1933, recommending that women be eligible for eldership but not ministry. It also commended the corresponding membership proposal as a temporary measure, pending a final decision on the eldership. These recommendations were referred to presbyteries but failed to secure the necessary support, and the matter was quietly dropped.

In September 1939 Britain found itself again at war, and the following May the General Assembly appointed a Special Commission, convened by Professor John Baillie, 'for the Interpretation of God's Will in the Present Crisis'. During those dark years the Commission presented a series of reports and, in the context of the role of women, it is relevant to note that the 1944 report included a recommendation that women should be eligible for the eldership. Baillie's rationale was that if the Church sought to offer guidance to the nation in a time of crisis, then it should be prepared to put its own house in order. After all, many women were working long hours on the land and in factories, contributing enormous value to the war effort. The Commission's proposal was referred to presbyteries, where it found support by a margin of 39 to 27. However, when this was reported in 1945 the Assembly was persuaded to send the matter back with a specific instruction to consult with kirk sessions and congregations. On this second time of asking the answer was a complete reversal of the previous vote: 44 presbyteries were now opposed and only 22 in favour.

In 1957 a number of presbyteries submitted Overtures on the subject and a further, inconclusive, consultation followed. Things were, however, moving, and in the early 1960s the question was taken up by the recently formed Panel on Doctrine. It appears that the Committee on the Place of Women no longer had a place. Eventually, an Overture recommending that women be eligible for the eldership on the same terms and conditions as men was approved by the General Assembly of 1965 and remitted to presbyteries under the Barrier Act. The following year it was reported that 45 presbyteries were in support, with 17 opposed. This was more than enough for the Assembly to convert the Overture into a standing law of the Church. Welcoming this outcome the Panel's convener, Dr Roy Sanderson, declared: 'This entitles women to take their part along with men when the Church acts corporately taking counsel. This they will do not as delegates of women in the Church … but in virtue of their baptism and as representatives of the corporate membership of the Church.' While the first women elders were ordained within weeks of the 1966 Assembly, there are still a number of congregations where the eldership continues to be all male. At 31 December 2015, out of a total 29,690, elders 15,889 were women and 13,801 men.

Related to the question of women elders and, arguably, more significant both ecumenically and in terms of gender equality, is the question of women ministers. In 1963 the Assembly had received a petition from Mary Lusk (later Levison), a deaconess serving as Assistant Chaplain to Edinburgh University. Note that this was three years before the decision on women elders. The petition was heard at the Saturday afternoon session and, given the choice between the Lord High Commissioner's Garden Party and staying on for the debate, many chose the latter. The public gallery was well filled and such was the level of interest that the Moderator, Professor James Stewart, had to call for order, twice threatening to have the gallery cleared. The atmosphere, indeed, would have been much as during the William Robertson Smith case in 1880. Eventually the matter was put to a vote with three options: to approve, to reject, to remit to the Panel on Doctrine. It was the last of these that carried.

In 1967 a report was presented revealing lack of agreement within the Panel. The Convener, Dr John Heron, stated that they had not seen their task as making a specific recommendation on Miss Lusk's petition but, rather, setting out the various theological considerations for the guidance of the Church. In face of this neutral approach an amendment from the floor cut to the chase. This moved that the Principal Clerk and the Procurator 'be instructed to draft an Overture ... enabling women to be ordained to the ministry on the same terms and conditions as men'. This carried the day by 397 votes to 298. Later in the Assembly the draft Overture was duly produced, approved and sent to presbyteries under the Barrier Act. There it found the same level of support as for women elders, with 45 presbyteries in favour and 17 against. Thus the way was clear for the 1968 Assembly to open the ministry to women. The following year the Revd Catherine McConachie became the Kirk's first woman minister on her ordination and appointment by the Presbytery of Aberdeen to serve as Assistant Minister at St George's Tillydrone. In 1972 the Revd Euphemia Irvine became the first woman to be ordained and inducted as a parish minister when appointed to Milton of Campsie. At time of writing (2016), women comprise around one quarter of the ministry.

While not the Kirk's first woman minister, it was certainly Mary Lusk who opened that particular door. She was born in Oxford in 1923, where her father was a Church of Scotland chaplain. After St Leonard's School in St Andrews she returned to Oxford, where she graduated with first class honours in philosophy, politics and economics. From Oxford she proceeded to New College, Edinburgh, then on to post-graduate study at Heidelberg and Basle. In 1954 she represented the Church of Scotland at the Second Assembly of the World Council of Churches in Evanston, Illinois. That same year she was commissioned as a deaconess and appointed to St Michael's Church in Musselburgh. While women were not eligible for ordination, deaconesses could be licensed to preach (but not administer the Sacraments) and Mary was so licensed by the Presbytery of Dalkeith. In 1961 she moved to Edinburgh University as Assistant Chaplain and, as already noted, it was while in this role that she petitioned the 1963 General Assembly.

Used with permission of Church of Scotland   Used with permission of Church of Scotland

Mary Levison.   *Alison Elliot.*

In 1965 she married Fred Levison, minister at St Bernard's, Edinburgh. Shortly afterwards they moved to the Borders and Mary continued to be involved in church committee work. In 1978 she was herself ordained as Assistant Minister at St Andrew's and St George's, Edinburgh, with a particular responsibility for developing ministry among the shops and offices of the city-centre parish. In 1991 she became the first woman to be appointed a Chaplain to the Queen in Scotland. Something of her character can be gauged by the title of her book, *Wrestling with the Church.* She explained the title by observing: 'wrestling there has been, but that is surely a different thing from fighting and campaigning'. She died in 2011.

It was a matter of regret that Mary Levison was never appointed Moderator of the General Assembly, though she was nominated in 1993. It was not until 2004 that the first woman was elected to that role, Dr Alison Elliot, an elder at Greyfriars Kirk, Edinburgh and a former convener of the Church and Nation Committee. Dr Elliot was also the first elder to serve as Moderator since the sixteenth century. At time of writing, two female ministers have held the office – Dr Sheilagh Kesting, the Church's Ecumenical Officer, in 2007, and Dr Lorna Hood, Minister at Renfrew Old Parish Church, in 2013.

Ecumenical and Interfaith Relations

In 1910 a major international gathering was held in what is today the Kirk's General Assembly Hall, but at the time was home to the United Free Church Assembly. This was the World Missionary Conference, attended by delegates from Protestant Churches and Missionary Societies from around the world. It was an event that marked a significant milestone in the development of the Ecumenical Movement.

It will hardly have escaped the reader's notice that relations among Scotland's post-Reformation churches had more to do with rivalry than co-operation. Denominations split, new bodies emerged only to divide again – and this was within

Presbyterianism, never mind relations with the Episcopal Church, a gradually recovering Roman Catholic Church and other denominations. Little wonder that a natural concern of the 1910 Conference was that mission should present the Gospel, as distinct from any particular denominational culture.

In this spirit of common Christian purpose the Conference, attended by 1,200 delegates, mainly from North America and northern Europe, took place. Its great aspiration was to win the world for Christ within a generation, and implicit in that goal was the recognition that it could be achieved only by the Churches working together. However, within four years world war had broken out and to this day that objective remains unachieved. Nevertheless, results followed in further initiatives across national and denominational boundaries. Examples include an International Missionary Council held in Jerusalem in 1928 and a further gathering in Tambaram, India in 1938, which led to the formation of the Church of South India. That Church, inaugurated in 1947, brought together Anglicans, Congregationalists, Methodists and Presbyterians, with one of its first bishops being the Church of Scotland missionary, Lesslie Newbigin. In 1942 the British Council of Churches was established, with the Scottish minister, Dr Archie Craig, as its Secretary, and in 1948 a great Assembly drawn from 147 churches convened in Amsterdam. This was the founding Assembly of the World Council of Churches. G. D. Henderson, Professor of Ecclesiastical History at Aberdeen University, attended from the Church of Scotland. Writing of the experience, he recalls that as a student in 1910 he had acted as a steward at the Edinburgh Missionary Conference and describes Amsterdam, like Edinburgh, as 'epoch-making'. Professor Henderson and Dr Craig both went on to serve as Moderators of the General Assembly, Henderson in 1955 and Craig in 1961.

Over the second half of the century various ecumenical initiatives emerged. In the 1950s there were talks involving the Kirk, the Scottish Episcopal Church and the Church of England. While 1929 had seen a major reunification of Presbyterian denominations, the more substantial division between Presbyterian and Episcopalian polity remained. Was the next challenge to attempt a blending of these strands within a Reformed Kirk of Scotland? Could a Church function with both presbyteries and bishops? The proposal to explore this was accepted but little progress was made, not least because of hostility within sections of the Scottish media to the very idea of bishops in the Kirk.

Other initiatives followed, with conversations in the late 1960s and into the 1970s between the Church of Scotland and the Methodist Synods of Scotland and Shetland. Indeed, a Basis and Plan of Union was approved by the General Assembly of 1978. However, the arrangements were not acceptable to the Methodists. There were also talks with the Congregational Union of Scotland over a possible union. This time it was the Kirk that failed to agree the scheme that had been accepted by the Congregationalists. An initiative named the Multilateral Church Conversations proceeded over a period from the late 1960s to the early 1990s and involved five Scottish denominations with two others observing. This failed to deliver a united Church but friendships were formed, trust established and the participants were led to a greater understanding of traditions other than their own. Thereafter the Scottish Episcopal Church took the initiative with a process known as The Scottish Churches' Initiative for Union (SCIFU), which once again sought to reconcile presbytery and bishop but, again, without success. The plan was firmly rejected by the General Assembly of 2003, largely on the grounds that proposals to accommodate bishops within presbyteries were considered too bureaucratic. It is also appropriate to mention the ecumenical approach taken to serving the new town of Livingston. In 1966 the Church of Scotland, Scottish Episcopal, Methodist and United Reformed Church (Congregational Union up to 1972) combined in 'the Livingston Ecumenical Experiment'. This pioneered a combining of resources, including ministry, liturgy and buildings as the denominations worked together to serve the new town. The project has received mixed reviews. In time the word 'experiment' was changed to 'parish' and, at time of writing, the congregation continues as 'Livingston United Church'.

By the late twentieth century a whole new approach to ecumenism was emerging, namely, that the priority should no longer be a merging of all traditions into one super-church; rather, there should be both acknowledgement of and respect for difference. At the same time, there should be a new focus on denominations working together. This principle was not new and had been particularly enshrined in a declaration of a World Council of Churches Conference held at Lund in Sweden in 1952. The principle stated simply that churches should act together in all matters except those in which deep differences of conviction compel them to act separately. In this spirit fresh ecumenical agencies were formed across the British Isles in 1990 and the new body in Scotland was called Action of Churches Together in Scotland, usually referred to as ACTS. The name says it all, with the focus on co-operation rather than attempts to achieve organic union. The other big step enabled by this approach was the willingness of the Roman Catholic Church to accept full membership of these new agencies in Scotland, England Ireland and Wales, and of the overarching Churches Together in Britain and Ireland (CTBI).

Alongside these conciliar developments a number of symbolic, but important, ecumenical gestures were taking place. In 1961 the Moderator of the General Assembly, Dr Archie Craig – a man with strong ecumenical credentials – met Pope John XXIII in the course of a visit to Rome, the first such encounter ever. Afterwards Dr Craig expressed the hope that his visit had 'helped to create the beginnings of a climate for dialogue and to set ... a pattern of courtesy, sincerity and charity'. Indeed, it did, and two years later the Kirk was invited to send observers to the Second Vatican Council. In 1969 the General Assembly welcomed Father Jock Dalrymple as the first official Roman Catholic Visitor to the General Assembly, and in 1975 Archbishop Tom Winning accepted an invitation to address the Assembly. This was a major first, which the archbishop acknowledged in his speech. He asked, 'What do brothers say to one another after years – and in our case, centuries of silence? Surely,' he continued, 'they ask for forgiveness.' In a moving response the Moderator, Dr James Matheson, invited members of the Assembly to stand and say the doxology together: 'Glory be to the Father and to the Son and to the Holy Ghost, as it was in the beginning, is now and ever shall be, world without end, Amen.' A tangible expression of this breaking of silence was the setting up in 1977 of the Joint Commission on Doctrine, which over the intervening years has provided an invaluable forum for open Church of Scotland-Roman Catholic discussion on difficult and divisive issues. Occasional conferences under the general theme of 'healing of memories' have also helped build a more positive relationship between the two denominations.

In June 1982 Pope John Paul II visited Scotland and was warmly welcomed by that year's Moderator, Professor John McIntyre. The meeting took place in the quadrangle of Edinburgh's New College by the steps leading to the Kirk's Assembly Hall. While the location was entirely appropriate there was some wry amusement at the proximity of a large statue of John Knox. The previous month the General Assembly had received a petition from the Free Presbyterian Church urging that the meeting should not take place, but this found little support. Indeed, four years later, the 1986 General Assembly overwhelmingly approved an Overture from Dr Kenneth Stewart, an elder from Stirling, which asked the Assembly to disassociate itself from the more intemperate language used in the Westminster Confession to refer to the Roman Catholic Church and the Pope. Such expressions, Dr Stewart successfully argued, were 'beyond modification except by their exclusion'.

Fast-forward to 2016, when Dr Justin Welby, Archbishop of Canterbury addressed the Assembly and spoke to The Columba Declaration, an ecumenical agreement between the Church of Scotland and the Church of England. The Kirk and the Church of England have very different systems of government but have a common role as national churches, albeit exercised in differing ways. The Church of England is an Established Church with a close relationship with the State. For example, twenty-six bishops sit as 'Lords Spiritual' in the House of Lords and the Sovereign is Supreme Governor of the Church. For many years a biennial consultation between the two Churches has been held, alternately north and south of the border. This brings together senior representatives to discuss matters of common interest. The Columba Declaration, approved by both Churches, builds on this and proclaims a statement of intent:

- Affirm and strengthen the relationship at a time when it is likely to be particularly critical in the life of the United Kingdom;
- Provide an effective framework for co-ordinating present partnership activities and for fostering new initiatives;
- Enable the two Churches to speak and act together more effectively in the face of the missionary challenges of our generation.

This UK-wide relationship reflects the national church roles played by both denominations. Meanwhile, the Kirk and the Scottish Episcopal Church continue to work ecumenically through a working group entitled Our Common Calling. This was established in 2016 with the express intention of strengthening relations.

Alongside engagement with other Christian denominations the Kirk has increasingly sought dialogue with other faith communities in Scotland. In 1984 Dr Henry Tankel, President of the United Synagogues of Scotland, became the first Jew to address the General Assembly. He spoke of 'a common belief in

the one God, our mutual respect for human rights and dignity
… our mutual desire for peace and our understanding of the
importance of spiritual values in a material world.' It should
also be noted that the Moderator of the General Assembly is, *ex
officio*, a President of the Council of Christians and Jews, along
with the Chief Rabbi and the Archbishop of Canterbury.

In 1993 the Assembly received a major report on Interfaith
Relations. Its thrust was to encourage engagement with people
of other faiths and to do so in the spirit of the San Antonio
Declaration. This statement, from a World Council of Churches
Consultation held at San Antonio in 1989, declared that as
Christians 'we cannot point to any other way of salvation
than Jesus Christ; at the same time we cannot set limits to the
saving power of God'. There are echoes here of the 1879 United
Presbyterian Declaratory Act on the Westminster Confession,
which stated that, in subscribing to the Confession, it was not
required to be held 'that God may not extend his grace to any
without the pale of ordinary means as may seem good in his
sight'. Indeed, when the reporting convener, Margaret Forrester,
was challenged for giving credence to other faiths, she referred
to the Declaratory Act and its place as a 'leading document' in
point of doctrine within the constitution of the Church. More
recently, Assembly reports in 2013 and 2014, have commended
an approach to interfaith relations in a spirit of admitting what
is good in other faiths without fear that we are diminishing our
own.

The 1993 report was very much in tune with the times,
which saw the emerging of bodies such as the Scottish Interfaith
Council and the Churches' Agency on Interfaith Relations. The
coming of the Scottish Parliament in 1999 also provided a focus
through the question of whether the Westminster pattern of
prayers should be replicated at Holyrood. At Westminster formal
Anglican prayers are led by a duty chaplain. What would happen
in Scotland, if anything? The outcome of the ensuing consultation
was agreement that there should be a Time for Reflection at the

start of each Parliamentary session. This would be arranged through the Presiding Officer's office, with contributors drawn from Scotland's Churches, faith communities and life stances. Frequency of invitation would be based on membership, something once referred to, archly, as 'proportional prayer'. Also associated with the Scottish Parliament was the creation of the Scottish Churches' Parliamentary Office. This was established on an ecumenical basis with a remit to facilitate liaison between the churches and Parliament.

The dreadful events of 9/11 provided a further stimulus to interfaith efforts. One particular initiative was the setting up of a Faith Leaders Meeting, held twice a year and hosted in turn by the various faith communities. From the start the Kirk has remained committed to this and to participation in an annual meeting of faith leaders with the First Minister. In 2010 Professor Mona Siddiqui became the first Muslim to address the General Assembly.

Iona

The tiny island of Iona has an iconic place in Scottish history. It was there in 563AD that Columba made landfall from Ireland and he and his attendant monks began their work of Christian evangelism using the natural transport network of sea and sea lochs. Columba also established a scriptorium for the production of illuminated sacred texts and it is highly possible that the Book of Kells originated in Iona before being taken for safety to Dublin. Beautifully carved stone crosses are also to be found on the island. Today little remains of the Columban settlement, swept away by Viking raids and Atlantic storms. In the Middle Ages more substantial buildings were erected by Benedictine monks and Iona also became home to a community of Augustinian nuns. In the seventeenth century Charles I declared the Abbey to be the diocesan Cathedral of the Isles and ordered restoration work to that end. However, by the end of the century the Abbey was again falling into a state of disrepair. For the next 200 years it would become a romantic ruin. Visiting Iona in 1773, Dr Samuel Johnson observed : 'That man is little to be envied, whose patriotism would not gain force upon the plain of Marathon, or whose piety would not grow warmer among the ruins of Iona.'

In 1899 the eighth Duke of Argyll, knowing he did not have long to live, set up a trust in connection with the Church of Scotland with a view to securing and restoring those self-same ruins. By 1913 the trustees, through major fundraising efforts supported by the Church, the Woman's Guild and other well-wishers, had restored the Abbey Church. The next phase in the story followed in the 1930s and involved the dynamic and charismatic George MacLeod, minister of Govan Old Parish Church, Glasgow. MacLeod was deeply concerned that the Church was not engaging effectively with working people and the poorer sections of society. It was also apparent to him that training for the ministry was largely academic, and that many candidates had no experience of working alongside tradesmen and labourers. The idea of creating a residential community was forming in his mind, and he was familiar with Iona from childhood holidays in Mull. A proposal was eventually put to the trustees, who gave it their blessing. This was to restore the monastic buildings, which still lay in ruins alongside the restored Abbey. The work would be undertaken during the summer months by tradesmen, with trainee ministers as their labourers. As unemployment was high this provided work for skilled men and allowed budding ministers to acquire some experience of manual labour. During their time on Iona they would live as a community and from this emerged the Iona Community, founded in 1938. MacLeod resigned his charge at Govan to devote himself entirely to its leadership.

Inevitably, there were those who demurred. MacLeod's evident socialism and his 'high church' tendencies led to the jibe that he was 'half-way between Rome and Moscow'. There were also tensions with the trustees over alterations MacLeod wanted in their restored Abbey Church. Then there were issues around the nature of the Community itself. An article in the *Scotsman* in June 1939 commented that women had been reading with interest of the life of the new Iona Community and were wondering where they fitted in. MacLeod, who would have been equally content with the designation 'Iona Brotherhood', pointed out that only men could be ministers and, of course, the tradesmen were also male. That was then and today's Community is fully inclusive, having had both male and female leaders. Work continued, and by 1945 the chapter house, library and refectory walls had been restored.

Iona Abbey.

Finally, it should be noted that in 2000 the Cathedral Trustees entered into a long-term lease of the Iona heritage to Historic Scotland (rebranded Historic Environment Scotland in 2015), which body now attends to its care and maintenance. The Trust's membership has been adjusted ecumenically to include the Roman Catholic and Scottish Episcopal Bishops of Argyll and the Isles and also a representative of the island Community Council. Freed of the pressures of constant fund-raising to maintain the ancient heritage, the Trust has taken on a new charitable purpose 'to advance the education of the public in relation to the history, culture and heritage of Iona Cathedral and the island of Iona'.

It may be helpful to clarify the references to both Iona Abbey and Iona Cathedral. Today's buildings comprise the restored Benedictine Abbey that replaced Columba's original settlement in the twelfth century. As noted, Charles I favoured the term 'Cathedral' and, in setting up his Trust in 1899, the Duke of Argyll used that term. Certainly George MacLeod preferred the term 'Abbey', and 'Iona Abbey' is the designation most commonly used today.

Relationship and Sexuality Issues

In 1959 the General Assembly passed legislation that authorised ministers to officiate at marriages where one, or both, of the parties were divorced and their former spouse still alive. Today such a provision seems less than radical but, at the time, it was a very significant change in church policy. No minister was required to go against conscience and sensitive inquiry was to be made into the circumstances surrounding the breakdown of the former marriage. Possible scandal was also to be weighed; at the same time, before refusing to solemnise the new marriage a minister was to take into careful consideration the moral and spiritual effect of a refusal on the parties. Quite a balancing act!

More controversial and divisive for the Church of Scotland and for many other denominations has been the issue of same-sex relationships. The subject was a growing source of disagreement within the Church from the 1950s onwards, becoming particularly intense when it focused on homosexuality and the ministry.

By the 1950s the United Kingdom government was giving serious attention to the decriminalisation of homosexual acts between consenting adults in private. A committee comprising three women and twelve men was set up under the chairmanship of Sir John Wolfenden. Its remit also included issues relating to prostitution. The coyness of the time can be noted by an early decision, 'for the sake of the ladies', to refer to the two groups as Huntley and Palmers! The Committee's membership included two prominent members of the Kirk – Dr R. F. V. Scott, Moderator of the 1956 General Assembly and Minister of St Columba's Pont Street, London, and Mr James Adair, a former Procurator Fiscal for Glasgow. Wolfenden delivered its recommendations in September 1957. These supported the case for decriminalisation, which had been agreed by all but one member of the Committee, namely Mr Adair. Whether by coincidence or design, he was a commissioner to the 1958 General Assembly. When the matter was debated that year on the report of the Church and Nation Committee it emerged that the Committee had been deeply divided, though the majority was against Wolfenden's recommendations. Consequently the recommendation was that the Assembly regard the proposed legal changes as 'inopportune ... and as calculated to increase rather than diminish this grave evil'. Against this a counter-motion, encouraged by the minority within the Committee, asked the Assembly to agree that Wolfenden was 'a fair minded exposition' and to support its principal recommendation. When the vote was taken the Committee carried the day and the Church of Scotland became the only major Church to oppose the proposed change in the law.

Over subsequent decades homosexuality continued to be debated, initiated by reports from the Committee on Moral Welfare (1960s) and the Board of Social Responsibility (1980s). Matters came to a head in 1994 when two pieces of work remitted to separate agencies appeared in that year's Assembly reports. One was from the Board of Social Responsibility, which had again been asked to reflect on Christian attitudes to homosexuality; the other came from the Panel on Doctrine, which had been given a remit to report on the theology of marriage. The Social Responsibility report tended towards a rehearsal of traditional arguments. By contrast, a flavour of the Panel on Doctrine's thinking can be assessed by a suggestion that there might be a place within the Christian fellowship for a 'loving and faithful homophile partnership'. Given this divergence it was proposed that the General Assembly simply debate the issues and then refer the whole matter to the consideration of the wider Church; in other words, no substantive votes would be taken by the Assembly. Inevitably, this procedural move itself became a matter of fierce debate, with various points of order being raised. Nevertheless, the Assembly resolved to proceed in this way. The wider Church debate continued over the ensuing years, eventually leading to a major report accepted by the General Assembly of 2007 and entitled 'A Challenge to Unity: Same-Sex Relationships as an Issue in Theology and Human Sexuality'. This was drawn up by people from across the spectrum of opinion and an interesting aspect of its reception was that, when individuals from one side or the other sought to push the recommendations further in their favoured direction, a member of the reporting body known to be sympathetic to the mover's point of view urged restraint in the interests of unity.

Experience shows that in such matters of controversy what really focuses the mind of the Church is a specific case rather than a theological discussion. For example, back in the 1960s, notwithstanding the decision to admit women to the eldership, there was still resistance to opening the ministry to women. The Church might well have debated the matter for a further decade had it not been for the petition from Mary Lusk (Levison). Effectively, this shifted the debate from the detached consideration of a principle to an assessment of an individual who had a proven track record in effective, albeit non-ordained, ministry.

Something similar happened with the sexuality debate. In 2009 the congregation of Queen's Cross Church, Aberdeen, called Scott Rennie, Minister at Brechin Cathedral, to be their minister. Mr Rennie had had a successful ministry in Brechin, which no doubt weighed with the Queen's Cross nominating committee. That committee was also aware of his sexuality, and this information had been shared with church members before they voted on his appointment. When the call came before the Presbytery of Aberdeen, the Presbytery voted by a majority to uphold it and induct Mr Rennie to the charge. However, a minority entered a Dissent and Complaint against that decision and this came to the General Assembly in May. By a majority of 328 to 267 the Assembly resolved to allow the induction to proceed. In addition the Assembly appointed a Special Commission 'representative of the breadth and unity of the Church' to consult widely and to prepare a study on Ordination and Induction to the Ministry in light of the 2007 report and the Queen's Cross Case'. Meantime, a moratorium was imposed on any further appointments of openly gay ministers.

The Commission comprised nine members and was chaired by Lord Hodge, a judge and former Procurator (senior legal adviser) of the Church. Its report in 2011 contained three main elements: an analysis of the views of kirk sessions and presbyteries; an account of consultations with experts on genetic and biological factors in determining human sexuality; and anonymised personal stories of individuals personally affected by the debate who had met in confidence with the Commission. The Commission also recommended that ministers in a same-sex relationship already in the service of the Church should be free to move from one parish to another, notwithstanding the moratorium put in place two years earlier. With regard to the moratorium itself, the Commission offered the Assembly a choice between two 'trajectories'. The first of these envisaged the moratorium being made permanent, closing the debate down and addressing the 'pastoral and procedural implications' for openly gay ministers already in the service of the Church. The second option was to consider lifting the moratorium and addressing questions such as whether ministers in a civil partnership, who had made a lifelong commitment to their partner in a Church ceremony, might be acceptable. In this connection an interesting piece of feedback showed that only seven presbyteries appeared open to 'a minister in a same-sex relationship', with thirty-seven opposed. However, when the question was reframed to refer to 'a minister in a civil partnership' the response indicated twenty-four open to the prospect, with twenty opposed. Finally the Commission suggested that further work of a specifically theological nature was required, and proposed the appointment of a new Commission 'representative of the Church's theological understanding'.

After a full day of debate the 2011 Assembly decided by a majority of 351 to 294 to continue the discussion in terms of the second 'trajectory' and to appoint a Theological Commission. Over the next four years debate continued, leading to draft legislation agreed by the 2015 Assembly. This affirmed 'the historic and current doctrine of the Church in relation to human sexuality'. At same time the legislation acknowledged, crucially, that this was an area in which liberty of opinion should be allowed. On this basis it recommended that a minister in a same-sex relationship could be inducted to a parish, provided the kirk session had, at the commencement of the vacancy, indicated its openness to the possibility of such an appointment. This proposal was referred in the usual way to presbyteries and came back in 2016 having been approved by twenty-six presbyteries and voted down by nineteen. In one presbytery the vote had been tied. The Assembly duly enacted the measure, adjusting it further to include ministers in a same-sex marriage. This was in light of the Scottish Parliament's extension of the civil law on marriage in Scotland. At time of writing the Church has still to take a view on whether its ministers should be authorised to conduct such marriage ceremonies.

'Believe Your Faith. Let the Church proclaim the eternal verities.'

With these words Lord Reith, Lord High Commissioner to the 1968 General Assembly, issued a challenge, perhaps even an instruction, to the Church of Scotland. These were the 'swinging sixties', when the whole concept of 'eternal verities' felt very uncertain. Even bishops seemed to be undermining traditional beliefs. In his address Lord Reith particularly singled out John Robinson, Bishop of Woolwich, who had recently published a book called *Honest to God* in which he speculated over the nature of the virgin birth, the miracles and the resurrection.

In the course of the Assembly, J. K. S. Reid, Professor of Systematic Theology at Aberdeen University, responded to Lord Reith's challenge with the question: 'What faith and which verities?' Professor Reid recalled a case where a minister had been accused of preaching doctrines 'felt to be at variance with the standards of the Church' and yet it been difficult to pinpoint what these standards were and, consequently, to determine whether the minister's statements had deviated from them. Supporting Professor Reid, Dr Nevile Davidson, minister of Glasgow Cathedral, addressed the problem head-on by arguing that a Confession of Faith that does not completely reflect the theological thinking and Christian conviction of the Church is failing in its purpose, and this was now the position with the Westminster Confession. On three counts it failed: it could no longer be regarded as safeguarding sound doctrine; it was not the kind of document that could be offered to potential new members; and it could no longer be held up as a clear and unequivocal statement of the Church's faith. In light of these concerns, Reid and Davidson moved that the Panel on Doctrine be instructed to review the place of the Confession as the Church's subordinate standard, a place it had held for over three centuries.

In the course of the same debate the Assembly received an Overture from Glasgow Presbytery along similar lines, but with a different thrust. The Presbytery's concern was not so much with the Church's doctrinal statements as such, but with the fact that they were very difficult for church members to access. Elders on their ordination were required to sign a formula the first sentence of which read: 'I believe the fundamental doctrines of the Christian Faith contained in the Confession of Faith of this Church.' As far back as the 1880s concern had been expressed that very few elders had ever read the Confession of Faith. By the 1960s it was unlikely that the number would have increased! The two proposals were, in effect, complementary. Reid and Davidson wanted a thorough reassessment of the status of the Westminster Confession; the Presbytery of Glasgow wanted an accessible statement of the Church's beliefs. Following debate, both concerns were remitted to the Panel on Doctrine and would engage the mind of the Church over the next six years.

One idea considered was the preparation of a new Confession of Faith altogether. However, the Panel suggested that 'it was doubtful whether such an attempt would be wise in this period of ecumenical change and theological ferment'. Another option was to depart altogether from the concept of a subordinate standard and prepare a brief statement of fundamental doctrines. These would then be inserted into the Preamble read at services of ordination and induction. That might have been acceptable but there was a trade-off, namely that the clause affirming liberty of opinion on matters not entering into the substance of the faith would be dropped. This eventually proved too high a price.

With regard to the position of the Westminster Confession, the eventual proposal was that its status should be reclassified. No longer should it be described as 'subordinate standard'; rather, it should be defined as a 'Historic Statement of the Reformed Faith'. Questions were raised as to whether it was within the power of the Church to make such a change, thereby resurrecting all the old arguments about the Church's freedom to vary doctrinal standards without the risk of challenge in the civil courts. The Procurator of the time, W. R. Grieve QC, was firm in his opinion that the Church would be exercising a legitimate freedom were it to go down such a road.

The mechanism for making changes was by amendment of the Articles Declaratory. Right from the start it had been felt important to consult presbyteries at every step of the way and by 1972 this process had led the Panel to prepare an Overture designed to give effect to the necessary changes to the Articles. The procedure was akin to the Barrier Act, though more rigorous in that a two-thirds majority of presbyteries was required in two successive years. Following the 1972 Assembly, forty-three presbyteries indicated approval, with eighteen opposed. Having reached the two-thirds threshold, the Overture went down again and came back in 1974 with an even larger majority – forty-nine to twelve. It seemed as if patient consultation was bearing fruit. Compromises had been made along the way but, while unanimity had never been a likely prospect, a decent majority was achieved. Indeed, the four-to-one presbytery majority was replicated in the votes of presbytery members, which indicated 2,052 in favour and 586 against.

However, it was not to be. The present writer was a commissioner to the 1974 Assembly and still recalls the debate that went on into the evening. There was a predictable rerun of the legal arguments, supported by a contrary legal opinion to that of Procurator Grieve. This raised the spectre of another Free Church case putting at risk the whole property of the Church. In response the new Procurator, C. K. Davidson QC, shared his predecessor's opinion that the Church was acting entirely legally and, though a successful challenge along the lines of the Free Church case was not impossible, it was, in his view, highly improbable. To what extent the lateness of the hour, the thinness of the house (fewer than half of commissioners took part in the vote) or fear of legal challenge led to an outcome so contrary to the mind of the Church as expressed over the previous two years, we shall never know; perhaps it was a combination of all three. But we do know the result, namely that on the motion of Dr Andrew Herron, seconded by Dr Duncan Shaw, the Assembly resolved by a majority of 292 votes to 238 to 'depart from the matter until a new statement of faith is accepted by the General Assembly'.

Faced with the collapse of all its work, the Panel dutifully indicated a willingness to continue with the drafting of a new Confession of Faith. This was duly prepared and sent to presbyteries in 1976, but it fell between two stools, satisfying neither those who sought a dogmatic test of orthodoxy nor those who desired an accessible pastoral and teaching tool. Realising the impossibility of its task, the Panel sought and was granted release from it in 1978. However, the Assembly eventually returned to the matter and in 1992 a new Statement of Christian Faith was authorised for use in worship and teaching. This is printed inside the back cover of the 1994 *Book of Common Order* 1994 and is printed as an Appendix to this book.

Over the intervening years occasional attempts have been made to revisit the status of the Westminster Confession but there appears to be little appetite for this. Accordingly it continues as the Kirk's 'principal subordinate standard'.

Liturgy and Worship

In 1922 the General Assemblies of the Church of Scotland and the United Free Church, along with the Presbyterian Church in Ireland, recognised that the time had come for a new edition of the *Church Hymnary*. Five years later the *Revised Church Hymnary* duly appeared. At the same time further work was undertaken on the metrical psalms, leading to the *Scottish Psalter, 1929*. This offered psalm portions suitable for use in worship and provided common arrangements of tunes between *Hymnary* and *Psalter*. This led to the split page psalter, so familiar to those attending churches from the 1930s up to the 1970s. Some 192 psalm tunes were offered in alphabetical order by metre, including more adventurous settings 'in reports'; for example 'Aberfeldy' and 'Bon-Accord' and the hugely popular 'Invocation' and 'St George's Edinburgh'. In 1940 a new *Book of Common Order* was published, the first since Knox's version of 1562. This contained a range of material for Sunday worship, along with services for occasions such as Baptism, Holy Communion, marriages and funerals and ordination of elders. There were also prayers for the seasons of the Christian Year and a lectionary of Bible readings for every Sunday. Of course, this was provided, as distinct from prescribed, but it was an indicator of a growing sense of order, dignity and discipline, far removed from the extempore approach of previous centuries. In recognition of the bilingual nature of the Kirk, a Gaelic supplement was also published. Prayers were provided for both morning and evening service. This reflected the 11 a.m. and 6.30 p.m. pattern of the early and middle years of the century, when the term 'twicer' was applied to those who attended both. However, by the 1960s evening attendances were rapidly declining, with the finger of blame being pointed at BBC television's broadcasting of John Galsworthy's *Forsyte Saga*.

By this time pressure was growing for further hymn book revision and this led in 1973 to *The Church Hymnary Third Edition* (CH3). This adopted a different approach from its predecessors in a number of respects. Whereas previously there had been a clear separation between psalms and hymns, CH3 offered psalm portions listed as hymns, scattered throughout the book under appropriate themed sections. There was no specific section of hymns for children, these again being thematically placed. A number of musical commissions from leading Scottish composers were included, though some of these were deemed somewhat challenging for the average congregation. Old favourites like 'What a friend we have in Jesus' disappeared along with Lowell Mason's much-loved tune for 'The Lord bless thee and keep thee', traditionally sung at Baptisms. Such changes led to a demand for a supplement, which duly appeared under the title *Songs of God's People*. This included a range of popular and contemporary hymns such as 'Seek ye first the kingdom of God' and 'One more step along the world I go', resulting in tension between ministers, keen to innovate and more traditional organists who felt the tone of divine worship was being distinctly lowered. Meanwhile, more and more congregations were signing up to copyright arrangements that allowed them, on payment of the appropriate fee, to produce their own supplements to the hymnary. Praise-bands were also introduced, sometimes at an alternative service, in other cases replacing the organ at the 'main' service. The music resources of the Iona Wild Goose Group and the Taizé Community also became very popular, along with traditional African songs, particularly those reflecting the liberation theology of the apartheid era.

If CH3 proved controversial so did a new *Book of Common Order* introduced by the Committee on Public Worship and Aids to Devotion in 1979. The 1940 edition had begun with five orders for morning and evening service, followed by orders for services such as Holy Communion, Baptism and other occasions. However, the 1979 edition opened with three services for Holy Communion, followed by an outline order for 'the main Sunday Service when the Lord's Supper is not celebrated'. This approach reflected the Committee's view that the standard church service involved both Word and Sacrament and so should include Holy Communion. This, the Committee asserted, had been the view of the Reformers and was the centuries-old tradition of the universal Church. This may well have been the case, but it was not in accordance with the way Scottish practice had evolved. Certainly, by the late twentieth century a number of congregations were developing more frequent and less formal celebrations, though few offered a weekly Communion and even fewer included the Sacrament every Sunday within the main service.

On the subject of Holy Communion, reference should also be made to another sacramental development in the 1970s and 1980s, namely the admission of baptised children to the Sacrament. In 1979 the Committee on Public Worship and Aids to Devotion may have argued that sacramental observance was 'normative' but, in practice, a typical mid-century communion celebration was anything but normal when compared with the regular Sunday service. Many found it too formal, overly long in duration and quite exclusive. For example, regular worshippers who were not on the Communion Roll might turn up as usual, only to be met by dark-suited elders collecting communion cards, which they did not have. Where Sunday School children regularly attended the first part of the service and a 'Children's Address' was given, on a Communion Sunday they were either excluded altogether or the older children were brought in to observe the proceedings from the gallery.

In the early 1970s an Assembly Committee was set up to explore the meaning of church membership. Essentially, this sought to tease out the relationship between Baptism, Confirmation and Admission to Holy Communion. A study of statistics was revealing. For example, in the late 1950s and early 1960s some 50,000 infants were being baptised each year. By late 1970s and early 1980s, the point at which these former infants were due to attend First Communicants' classes, the annual number of admissions by Profession of Faith was around 14,000. That's quite a rate of attrition. While social factors came into play, there were also questions as to the quality and effectiveness of Christian nurture. The outcome of various discussions was a proposal brought to the 1982 Assembly to open the Lord's Table to baptised children, thereby signifying their membership of the Church through Baptism and the nurturing role of Holy Communion for all who seek to grow in faith. The proposal was accepted by the Assembly but, in recognition of the change in practice, it was sent to presbyteries under the Barrier Act. There it fell, with twenty presbyteries in favour but twenty-eight against. However, in 1989 the matter was revisited. Fresh proposals were brought to the Assembly of 1991, where they were approved and subsequently endorsed by a majority of presbyteries. The enabling legislation was enacted in 1992 and provides that 'where a Kirk Session is satisfied that baptised children are being nurtured within the life and worship of the Church and love the Lord and respond in faith to the invitation "take, eat", it may admit such children to the Lord's Table ...' The annual statistical return to the General Assembly of 2016 showed that 3,090 children had received Holy Communion the previous year.

Under this section on liturgy and worship, brief reference should also be made to a controversy that rocked the Kirk during the 1980s. At the 1982 meeting of the Woman's Guild the National President, Anne Hepburn, offered the following prayer composed by Brian Wren: 'Dear Mother God, you give birth to all life and love us to the uttermost. Your love surrounds us and feeds us. Within your love we find our home, our joy, our freedom. You open the world to us and give us room to grow and change ... Help us, dear Mother God, to catch something of your love.' Unsurprisingly, this raised more eyebrows than heaven-bound petitions, and when the General Assembly met in May, questions were raised. The outcome of a tense debate was a decision to invite the Guild to set up a study group to consult with the Panel on Doctrine on the theological implications of the concept of the Motherhood of God and report to a subsequent General Assembly. The report appeared two years later and was duly presented to the Assembly of 1984, where it was not well received. Indeed, such was the hostility that it was not received at all, a very unusual response to a piece of work commissioned by a previous General Assembly. The report reflected on the nature of God as being above human gender distinctions and drew attention to a whole range of biblical images of God other than 'father', including the mother image, as in Isaiah 66:13. It also reflected on how, down the centuries, Christians had drawn on a rich history of reflection on the mystery and majesty of the divine being. As is so often the way in these situations, the effect of such out and out dismissal was to heighten the publicity surrounding the report and encourage a worldwide interest in its analysis and conclusions.

In 1994 a fourth *Book of Common Order* was published, just fifteen years after its predecessor. Generally known by the abbreviated title, *Common Order*, this edition reverted to the pattern of the 1940 book, with a range of services for morning and evening worship followed by orders for special occasions. Communion services were included in this latter category. The Christian Year continued to feature strongly, with a lectionary and prayers for the various seasons and festivals. A new feature was a note on liturgical colours for banners and pulpit falls – purple for Advent and Lent, white for Christmas and Easter, red for Pentecost, green for 'ordinary time'. Whereas mid-century ministers invariably wore black cassock, Geneva gown and academic hood, by the end of the century various shades of cassock were appearing, with additional colour provided by clerical stoles and preaching scarves. Others chose to dispose of robes altogether, preferring to wear more everyday dress when leading worship.

The 1994 *Common Order* was followed in 2005 by a fourth edition of the *Church Hymnary* (CH4). This recovered specific reference to the Psalter, with the first 108 entries being verses from the psalms. It should be added that these were not all from the Scottish metrical psalter, though the most popular of these were included. Also featured were some of the old favourites dropped from CH3 and a great number of new hymns, in contemporary style, which had become popular through *Songs of God's People*. Also, initially controversial but becoming more accepted, there was a policy of adjusting some of the language of traditional hymns to remove archaic or exclusive language. In 'Jesus shall reign' worshippers no longer bring 'peculiar' but 'highest honours' to the king. Meanwhile, 'Rise up, O men of God' has disappeared altogether. It should also be noted that, notwithstanding the 1982 controversy, both CH4 and *Common Order* 1994 include material that refers to God as Mother.

Mission and Evangelism

The middle years of the century saw a major initiative in evangelism through the formation of the Tell Scotland movement. This joint initiative by seven of Scotland's Protestant churches grew out of various local campaigns led by ministers such as David Patrick Thomson (always known as 'DP') and Tom Allen. Eventually Allen demitted his charge at North Kelvinside to become full-time Field Organiser of the movement. Another prominent figure was George MacLeod, a strong believer in the congregation as the primary agent of mission who involved the Iona Community in parish missions in support of new congregations in post-war housing schemes. Indeed, such church extension work was a major plank in church policy in the 1950s and 1960s, as it had been in the 1930s under John White.

A particularly high-profile enterprise was Billy Graham's All Scotland Crusade, held in Glasgow in the spring of 1955. The previous year Graham had conducted a similar event in London with much success, and this led to a Tell Scotland invitation to come north. Not all were in favour, with particular resistance from George MacLeod, who feared that Graham's approach would undermine the parish outreach of congregations. In the event the invitation was issued and accepted. Large crowds attended rallies in Glasgow's Kelvin Hall and came forward to accept Christ. Tom Allen, who chaired the Crusade Executive Committee, reported that almost 1.2 million people had been reached. Inevitably, not all went on to a lifelong commitment but many did, including a number who responded to a call to the ministry.

Interdenominational follow-up campaigns were conducted around Scotland. These involved door-to-door visitation aimed at connecting people touched by the Crusade with a local congregation. These efforts were complemented by a series of Tell Scotland campaigns throughout the late 1950s led by D. P. Thomson and Tom Allen, and it is perhaps no coincidence that communicant membership of the Church of Scotland hit an all-time high of 1.3 million during this period. However, such energy levels are not indefinitely sustainable. By 1964, Tell Scotland had become the Department of Mission of the new Scottish Churches' Council; but initiatives continued. That year the present writer took part in a 'Summer Mission' to the new town of Cumbernauld, led by the Scottish Churches Student Team. This involved a cross-faculty group of around thirty students spending the last two weeks of September camping in church halls and working with the local ministers and congregations. Door-to-door visitation, youth work, participation in church services, contributing to school assemblies all featured on the programme of helping to build up the young churches of the new town.

In 1955 Tom Allen was appointed minister of St George's Tron in Glasgow. From there he developed a wider ministry through newspaper articles and broadcasting. He was also involved in setting up counselling and rehabilitation services that continue under his name, working also with the Glasgow Lodging House Mission in support of people who were homeless and facing other vulnerabilities. In 1958, D. P. Thomson opened the St Ninian's Centre in Crieff. Over the next half-century, St Ninian's would host residential conferences for groups of all ages and contribute richly to the life of congregations around Scotland. However, by the turn of the century changing expectations of conference facilities led the 2001 Assembly to accept proposals to close St Ninian's, though not without a strong campaign of resistance.

By the late twentieth century the Kirk was prioritising its work, and a major report discussed at the 1995 General Assembly argued for two principal priorities: parish staffing and congregational resourcing (ensuring congregations were well equipped to carry out their local witness and mission). This was not to exclude other work, though a fierce reaction came from those fearing the Church was abandoning its responsibilities to the worldwide Church. A turf war developed as various agencies sought to protect their own budgets, while those charged with overall management drew attention to the limited nature of financial resources. Eventually these negotiations led to a significant overhaul of the central administration. It can be noted, though, that the focus on ministries and congregational resourcing was, in effect, a reaffirmation of the congregation as primary agent of mission. The message was that the strength of a denomination lies not in its central structures but in the calibre of its congregations.

This thinking led to the setting up of a Special Commission on Review and Reform, chaired by Peter Neilson, a minister with a proven track record in mission and evangelism. This delivered a report entitled *Church Without Walls* to the General Assembly of 2001. The catchy title caught on and inspired a range of new initiatives aimed at engaging with the wider community beyond the walls of the Church. A key thrust was to encourage members to think of themselves not so much as part of an organisation but as disciples of Jesus Christ. The primary focus of the Church was outlined as, first, to follow Jesus Christ as Lord; second, to share in Christ's mission in the world; and third, to turn back to God and neighbour. The report also called for a root-and-branch review of the Kirk's central structures, with a greater focus on equipping the whole membership for mission and service.

By 2004 a new slimmed-down central administration was in place. This involved five Councils: Church and Society; Ministries; Mission and Discipleship; Social Care; and World Mission. Along with this went an overarching Council of Assembly, with the authority to co-ordinate, support and evaluate the central organisation. The plural 'ministries' signalled a range of forms alongside the traditional parish ministry. In part this was a response to declining ministerial recruitment; but it also reflected a growing recognition of the value of 'other ministries' specialising in areas such as children's and youth work, pastoral care, community development and Christian education. Also, as part of the follow-up to *Church Without Walls* a series of well-attended conferences was held, led by Albert Bogle, a parish minister in Bo'ness and future Moderator, who had established a reputation for innovative thinking. This in turn led to an engagement with new initiatives being pioneered by other denominations. These included 'Fresh Expressions', 'Emerging Church' and 'Messy Church'. For example, it was increasingly apparent that the Church could no longer claim a monopoly on Sunday mornings. Parents who may have attended Sunday School as children now came under pressure to let their own children participate in mini-rugby, football training, biking clubs and similar ventures with which traditional Sunday School just could not compete. Messy Church, by contrast, sought to offer, say, a monthly Sunday afternoon session with play, arts and crafts along with Bible teaching and songs, and concluding with pizza. Meanwhile, in communities across Scotland the potential for the church complex to become a base for community projects, such as food banks, drop-in advice centres and friendship groups, was being developed.

In April 1994 some 250 young people from congregations around Scotland attended the first Youth Assembly and debated some of the issues scheduled for discussion at the following month's General Assembly. Further assemblies were held in 1997 and 2000, after which the gathering became an annual event. Since 1998 youth representatives have participated in the General Assembly itself, where they have the right to speak and move motions, though not to vote. Also deserving of mention is 'Heart and Soul'. This takes the form of a Christian festival in Edinburgh's Princess Street Gardens on the Sunday afternoon of Assembly Week. It offers an opportunity for congregations and church agencies to showcase their work in this very public arena, along with music and entertainment, worship and celebration, open to all.

Political and Social Engagement

In 1919 the General Assembly established a Church and Nation Committee and throughout the century its reports generated many lively and well-publicised debates. One of the Committee's earliest reports proved also to be one of its most controversial. The year was 1923 and the tenor of the report can immediately be judged from its title: 'The Menace of the Irish Race to our Scottish Nationality'. The Committee, under the convenership of Dr John White, expressed concern at what it saw as the undermining of Presbyterian values through drunkenness, crime and financial imprudence. It specifically called for an end to Irish Catholic immigration and the deportation of those convicted of a criminal offence or living on state benefits. Meanwhile, the Orange population of Scotland was affirmed as being 'of the same race as ourselves and of the same Faith and already assimilated to the Scottish race'.

Certainly immigration from southern Ireland had increased over previous decades, adding members to a reviving Roman Catholic Church. The Scottish hierarchy had been restored in 1878 and the provisions of a 1918 Education Act included state funding of Roman Catholic Schools. The Irish Free State had emerged in 1922 and memories of the 1916 Easter Rising were recent. Post-war failure to deliver 'a land fit for heroes' promised by the Lloyd George government would also have been a factor with, as ever, immigrants an easy target in times of economic uncertainty. At the same time there is evidence that before and during the First World War relationships between the Irish and indigenous populations of Scotland had been improving. Also, in the first decade of the century both the Kirk and the United Free Church had placed great emphasis on the social Gospel, with a strong commitment to tackling issues such as homelessness and unemployment. The 1923 report thus represented a change of tone and, sadly, gave cover to a culture in which a standard interview question inquired as to which school the applicant had attended. Today it makes deeply embarrassing reading, which is why, in the course of a 2002 debate on sectarianism, the General Assembly disassociated itself from it and affirmed its support for future moves towards a more tolerant society.

As already noted, in May 1940 the General Assembly

appointed a Special Commission, convened by Professor John Baillie, 'for the Interpretation of God's Will in the Present Crisis'. During those dark wartime years the Commission presented a series of reports, and reference has already been made to its call for women to be admitted to the eldership. These reports offered both breadth and depth as they engaged with a range of issues – theological, ecclesiastical, political and domestic. For example, the 1944 report commended the benefits of artificial methods of birth control to young married couples. It also called for public control of capital resources and means of production, the revitalisation of democracy, the eradication of the evils of colonialism and the general improvement of the international order.

Throughout the 1970s and 1980s a recurring topic at the General Assembly was Britain's possession of nuclear weapons, with George MacLeod, by then Lord MacLeod of Fuinary, the arch-advocate for their abolition. One of MacLeod's last Assembly appearances was in 1986 when, at the age of ninety-one, he moved the following motion: 'As of now the General Assembly declare that no Church can accede to the use of nuclear weapons to defend any cause whatever. They call on Her Majesty's Government to desist from their use and from their further deployment.' In those Cold War days MacLeod was listened to with respect but never carried the vote; but something changed that year, the year of the Chernobyl nuclear catastrophe. A regular opponent of MacLeod was a retired colonel from Elie, G. N. Warnock, who stoutly defended the deterrent argument. However, this year Warnock rose not to oppose but to support MacLeod. As people sat up and listened, they heard him saying that Chernobyl had changed everything and now, if he were still a serving soldier and were ordered to press the nuclear button, he would not be prepared to do it; he would shoot himself first. In the verbatim minutes of that day Warnock's speech is followed by '(Applause'). MacLeod's motion carried and remains the policy of the General Assembly.

On 21 May 1988 Margaret Thatcher addressed the General Assembly as Prime Minister. She was present, not at the invitation of the Assembly, but as a guest of that year's Lord High Commissioner, and the convention is that when a particularly distinguished guest is present in the Throne Gallery, he or she is invited by the Moderator to address the Assembly.

Mrs Thatcher took the opportunity to offer a theological rationale of her political and economic theories. This led the media, mindful of the location of the Assembly Hall, to refer to her address as 'the Sermon on the Mound'. The Prime Minister even had a text from 2 Thessalonians: 'if a man will not work he shall not eat'. In light of recent closures of steel works and a general decline in Scottish heavy industry, this did not play particularly well with the Assembly. Indeed, recent reports of the Church and Nation Committee had been critical of aspects of government policy and there was a sense that the Prime Minister was keen to set the record straight. The Assembly listened courteously and when she had concluded her speech the Moderator, Professor James Whyte, thanked her and presented her with a copy of the 'Blue Book' (the volume of Assembly reports). In doing so he drew particular attention to reports on housing and poverty. There were smiles at the mention of the Blue Book and the highlighting of the particular reports was interpreted by the media as a polite rebuke.

In 2004 the Church and Nation Committee was rebranded the Church and Society Council, taking on the social and moral welfare remit of the former Board of Social Responsibility. This enabled that body to concentrate on the practical delivery of social care. Since 2005 this long-established church-based work has been carried out under the name 'CrossReach' which, with over 2,000 staff, is one of the country's largest providers of care services. These include care for older people, help with alcohol, drug and mental health problems and assistance for homeless people and those with special learning needs. Although part of the Church of Scotland and delivering care 'in Christ's name',

CrossReach services are open to people of all faiths and none.

In 2001 the General Assembly declared that 'priority for the poorest and most marginalised is the Gospel imperative facing the whole Church and not just the Church in poorest communities'. This led to the identification of areas where a church presence in the community was extremely fragile due to multiple levels of deprivation. Evidence indicates that across Western Europe, church decline is particularly marked in the poorest communities a similar pattern can be seen in deprived areas of Scotland. Accordingly, the Priority Areas Committee supports a range of activities that are particularly designed to help local congregations share the Gospel in relevant and inspirational ways, leading to growth and deepening of faith.

Thomas Chalmers would certainly have agreed that enabling effective ministry in such communities was a responsibility for the whole Church. However, it will be recalled that Chalmers tended to view social problems essentially as a sign of moral failure and religious neglect, matters that were primarily for the Church to address. By contrast, today's approach, building on a tradition of social and political engagement, is recognised as being not for the Church alone, but rather through the forging of partnerships with secular agencies. Today's Priority Areas Committee believes that the real problem is not poverty, but wealth and an inability to share it. This, in itself, is a political statement which calls for engagement with secular policy makers and legislators. In the words of the 2014 Assembly report: 'We have a responsibility to recognise what it is that causes poverty in the first place, and to call for change in the way our current economic system creates poverty.' Other agencies active in this area include the Scottish Churches Housing Association and Fresh Start, which work specifically to help people out of homelessness. Many congregations also support the provision of food banks in their communities.

It would be remiss for this section on social and political engagement to make no mention of one of the main issues in

Scottish debate over the later years of the twentieth century and into the twenty-first, namely the question of Scotland's place within the United Kingdom and Europe.

In 1989, the year after Margaret Thatcher's 'Sermon on the Mound', there emerged a body called the Scottish Constitutional Convention. This developed from an earlier Campaign for a Scottish Assembly, which had been set up following the failure of a 1979 referendum to deliver a devolved Scottish Assembly. Throughout the 1980s the Campaign kept up pressure for some measure of home rule, and in 1988 it produced a Claim of Right for Scotland. This contended, on the basis of the 1320 Declaration of Arbroath, that it was the right of the Scottish people to choose the form of government that best suited them. The very term 'Claim of Right' had a powerful historical resonance, having been used by the pre-Disruption Kirk in 1842 and the Scottish Parliament in 1689. In 1989 this latest Claim of Right led to the setting up of the Scottish Constitutional Convention, which took forward the work of the Campaign for a Scottish Assembly. The Convention first met in the General Assembly Hall on 30 March 1989. There was Church representation, including the Church of Scotland and the Roman Catholic Church. Some but not all political parties participated, along with the Scottish Trades Union Congress, the Council for Development and Industry and other groups from civic society. Canon Kenyon Wright of the Scottish Episcopal Church served as executive chairman, and on St Andrew's Day, 1990, the Convention published its proposals for a legislature, elected by proportional representation and with powers to raise taxes in Scotland. Throughout this process the General Assembly expressed its support for the principle of home rule.

In 1997 a second referendum was held. This time the vote was in favour of a devolved Scottish Parliament with tax-raising powers. On 1 July 1999 the Scottish Parliament duly re-convened in the General Assembly Hall, in the presence of the Queen and Duke of Edinburgh. The ceremony opened with the singing of the hundredth psalm and also included Scottish folk singer Sheena Wellington singing Robert Burns' 'A man's a man for a' that'. By the time she reached the final verse everyone was singing along. For the next few years, while the new Holyrood building was under construction, the Parliament continued to meet in the Assembly Hall.

While the General Assembly was prepared to express its support for devolution, it declined to express a view on the 2014 independence referendum. Some thought this was wise; others were disappointed. The Church, though, was active in a non-partisan way through the publication of a report entitled 'Imagining Scotland's Future'. In the run-up to the referendum a range of church-hosted events took place across the country. These focused on the values people considered most important for the future and how they might be harnessed to make Scotland a better place. On the Sunday after the referendum the Moderator, John Chalmers, preached at a 'Service Reflecting Shared Values and Common Purpose' in St Giles' Cathedral. This was attended by politicians, ecumenical representatives and civic leaders and broadcast worldwide. In a powerful symbolic act leaders from the five parties represented in Parliament came

Used with permission of Church of Scotland

Political leaders at the post-referendum service.

forward, each holding a lighted taper, and together lit a single candle.

In June 2016 another referendum was held throughout the United Kingdom. The question this time was whether to remain in or leave the European Union. In the 1980s the General Assembly had expressed its support for Scottish devolution; in 2014 it declined to take sides in the independence debate. How would it respond to the European referendum? Well, on this occasion the Assembly did nail its colours to the mast by affirming the work of the European Union in promoting peace, security and reconciliation, expressing its belief that the UK should remain a member and calling for institutions that support the rights and well-being of the Union's poorest citizens.

What Now for the Kirk?

A wise historian was asked to predict the consequences of a particular series of events. Back came the reply: 'the future is not my period'. We might also recall Burns' lines: 'forward tho' we canna see we guess an' fear'. After all, extrapolators are already working on the membership statistics to pinpoint the exact date when the last church member will put out the lights. Alternatively, we might take courage from a popular hymn by Andrew Scobie, sung to the rousing tune, 'Cardross', named after the place where he ministered for forty-five years:

> Look forward in faith,
> all time is in God's hand.
> Walk humbly with him
> and trust his future plan.

As the twenty-first century unfolds the Kirk finds itself adjusting to a very different status to that of even the last quarter of the previous century. Its commitment to being a national Church was reaffirmed by the General Assembly of 2010, albeit with a subtle shift of emphasis. That reaffirmation did not describe the Church as 'representative of the Christian Faith of the Scottish people' (the original 1929 wording). Rather, it spoke of 'a national Church with a distinctive evangelical and pastoral concern for the people and nation of Scotland'. With reference to the 1921 Church of Scotland Act the 2010 Assembly declared that the Kirk's 'true origin and entire basis lie not in civil law but in the Church's own calling by Jesus Christ, its King and Head'. There are echoes of earlier conflicts here, but also a progressive and appropriate acknowledgement of a very different Scotland. In the spirit of the great Edinburgh Conference of 1910, the 2010 Assembly also expressed an ecumenical desire 'to share with other churches in Christian mission and service to the people of Scotland'. A Scotland-wide presence was pledged, though this will look rather different from a century ago when there was an ordained minister in every parish. For example, a report to the 2016 General Assembly envisaged a scenario whereby a single minister could be responsible for a team of locally based colleagues, with different gifts, skills and roles, serving upwards of a dozen congregations over a large geographical area.

The Kirk has maintained its cherished spiritual independence, but over the inter-century period it has had to adapt to a measure of secular scrutiny. It remains Scotland's largest charity, and the introduction of a more stringent regulatory regime, administered by the Office of the Scottish Charity Regulator (OSCR), has had implications for all charities, including the Church of Scotland. Every congregation is now a charity with its own charity number, and with the minister and elders acting as charity trustees. The elected members of the Council of Assembly act as charity trustees for the Kirk's central administration. These new arrangements were initially viewed with some concern, but the regulation and oversight is confined to the sphere of financial management and governance. Moreover, churches benefit from a Designated Religious Charity status, which means that, while still under the OSCR regime, the

Regulator does not have the power to remove church trustees, something that would have implications for membership of kirk sessions. This designated status gives the Church autonomy in the oversight of its constituent parts. At the same time that oversight is exercised in the full knowledge that religious charity status could be withdrawn.

Issues have arisen in relation to equality and employment law. Inducted parish ministers do not work under contract, but are holders of an ecclesiastical office, which does not meet the definition of an office-holder in equalities legislation. Thus, they do not have access to civil tribunals and, accordingly, the General Assembly has put in place its own procedures for dealing with any complaints they might make of bullying or discrimination. On the other hand, it has been held that associate ministers are employees with rights of access to civil tribunals. The same applies to non-ministerial employees of the Church and to ordained ministers working under contracts of employment. With regard to the ongoing debate on gay clergy, the law does allow for discrimination where there is a requirement to comply with the doctrines of a religion, or there is a need to avoid conflicting with the strongly held religious convictions of a significant number of the religion's followers. The Church is free to solemnise only marriages between a man and a woman but, as society changes and if the influence of the Church further diminishes, there is no guarantee that the Churches would not come under pressure to conform to the new civil extension of marriage, or relinquish the right to solemnise any marriage on behalf of the civil authority. For example, it has long been the practice in Germany and some other countries that the legal marriage ceremony is carried out by the civil authority with, for those who wish it, a service of church blessing following. Of course, questions might then arise were a minister to refuse to bless a same-sex marriage. Meanwhile, the Kirk has taken steps to facilitate the ordination and induction of ministers in civil partnerships and same-sex marriages where the kirk session, at the commencement of a vacancy, rules that such an appointment would be acceptable.

The issue of gay clergy has been a particularly divisive one, leading to the loss of a number of ministers and members. It remains to be seen whether this pattern will continue or, as effective ministries are exercised by gay men and women, this will cease to be an issue. Is there perhaps a parallel with congregations that in time past rejected the patron's nominee on principle, only to discover when they got to know him, what a fine minister he was? Thus far, it can be stated with some satisfaction that while, inevitably, there has been disagreement and division, the loss of membership has been less than some feared. After all, at one point there was speculation about another Disruption.

The Kirk, along with other denominations, cannot remain unaffected by changing social attitudes to religion. Perceived homophobia, reports of clergy abuse, various brands of mediaeval fundamentalism wreaking terror on people and destruction of heritage – such things bring religion into disrepute and faith finds itself on the back foot. Sadly, the history narrated in these pages includes violence and brutality in the name of religion, wrought by fundamentalist mindsets excoriating, excommunicating and executing one another over the merest jot and tittle. In the 1940s, when Professor Baillie reflected on 'God's will in the present crisis', he was careful to point out the Church's need to put its own house in order. Who would dare to say that task has been achieved? Perhaps, until it is, religion will continue to be seen as part of the problem rather than part of the solution of the human condition. Yet for all its flaws, the Kirk is still called to witness to the Gospel and point to Christ's simple, yet challenging commandment to love God and to love one's neighbour as oneself. When a passing lawyer asked for further clarification, he was rewarded with the parable of the Good Samaritan, in which the person who cared for the injured traveller came from a different tribe.

The history narrated in this book shows that there remains one major division in the Scottish post-Reformation Church, namely the separation into Presbyterian and Episcopalian. The Presbyterian splits following the 1690 settlement have largely, if not entirely, been healed, but the Kirk and the Scottish Episcopal Church continue as separate bodies, albeit in close ecumenical relationship. Back in the seventeenth century, Bishop Leighton of Dunblane was perfectly content to work in a hybrid environment, serving as permanent Moderator of the Presbytery while working collegially with his ministerial colleagues. Of course his contemporary, Archbishop Sharp, was an altogether different character. Leighton was the pastor, Sharp the prelate. A continuing issue for the Kirk is its continually changing leadership, with a new Moderator every year. In a media age many regard this as a lost opportunity. However, it would not be sufficient simply to appoint Moderators for longer. There would also need to be a review of the role in terms of powers and responsibilities vested in the office; but how far would one have to go down that road before the role started to look very like that of a bishop, or even an archbishop?

This book began with the Reformation and has sought to outline the Kirk's story over the five centuries since Martin Luther posted his Ninety-Five Theses in Wittenberg in 1517. We cannot tell how the story will continue into the future, but continue it surely will, so long as the Kirk remains committed to a continuing and positive process of reform and renewal.

A Statement of Christian Faith, Authorised for Use in Worship and Teaching by the General Assembly of 1992

We believe in one God:
Father, Son and Holy Spirit.
God is love.

We praise God the Father:
who created the universe and keeps it in being.
He has made us his sons and daughters to share his joy,
living together in justice and peace,
caring for his world and for each other.

We proclaim Jesus Christ, God the Son:
born of Mary, by the power of the Holy Spirit,
he became one of us, sharing our life and death.
He made known God's compassion and mercy,
giving hope and declaring forgiveness of sin,
offering healing and wholeness to all.
By his death on the cross and by his resurrection,
He has triumphed over evil.
Jesus is Lord of life and of all creation.

We trust God the Holy Spirit:
who unites us to Christ and gives life to the Church:
who brings us to repentance and assures us of forgiveness.
The Spirit guides us in our understanding of the Bible,
renews us in the sacraments, and calls us to serve God in the world.

We rejoice in the gift of eternal life:
we have sure and certain hope of resurrection through Christ,
and we look for his coming again to judge the world.
Then all things will be made new;
and creation will rejoice in worshipping the Father,
through the Son,
in the power of the Spirit,
one God, blessed for ever.
Amen.

BIBLIOGRAPHY AND
FURTHER READING

Aisthorpe, Steve, 2016, *The Invisible Church*, Edinburgh: Saint
    Andrew Press.
Bardgett, Frank, 2006, 'Missions and Missionaries: Home', in Colin
    MacLean and Kenneth Veitch (eds), *A Compendium of Scottish
    Ethnology*, Volume 12, *Religion*, Edinburgh: John Donald, an
    imprint of Birlinn.
Buchan, John, 1927, *Witch Wood*, London: Hodder & Stoughton.
Buchan, John, 1928, *Montrose*, Westport, CT: Greenwood Press.
Burleigh, J. H. S., 1960, A *Church History of Scotland*, London: Oxford
    University Press.
Cheyne, A. C., 1983, *The Transforming of the Kirk*, Edinburgh: Saint
    Andrew Press.
Cheyne, A. C., 1999, *Studies in Scottish Church History*, Edinburgh:
    T&T Clark.
Cameron, J. K. (ed.), 1972, *The First Book of Discipline*, Edinburgh:
    Saint Andrew Press.
Davidson, Julie, 2012, *Looking for Mrs Livingstone*, Edinburgh: Saint
    Andrew Press.
Dawson, Jane E. A., 2007, *Scotland Re-formed 1488–1587*, Edinburgh:
    Edinburgh University Press.
Dawson, Jane E. A., 2015, *John Knox*, New Haven, CT: Yale University
    Press.
Donaldson, Gordon, 1960, *The Scottish 1560 Reformation*,
    Cambridge: Cambridge University Press.
Donaldson, Gordon, 1980, *Scotland: The Shaping of a Nation*, Newton
    Abott: David & Charles.
Drummond, A. L. and J. Bulloch, 1973, *The Scottish Church 1688-
    1843*, Edinburgh: Saint Andrew Press.
Drummond, A. L. and J. Bulloch, 1975, *The Church in Victorian
    Scotland*, Edinburgh: Saint Andrew Press.

Drummond, A. L. and J. Bulloch, 1978, *The Church in Late Victorian Scotland*, Edinburgh: Saint Andrew Press.

Duke, John A., 1937, *A History of the Church of Scotland to the Reformation*, Edinburgh: Oliver & Boyd.

Dunlop, A. I., 1967, *William Carstares and the Kirk by Law Established*, Edinburgh: Saint Andrew Press.

Eire, Carlos, 2015, 'Calvinism and the Reform of the Reformation', in Peter Marshall (ed.), *The Oxford Illustrated History of the Reformation*, Oxford: Oxford University Press.

Galbraith, Douglas, 2006, 'Music, Church and People', in Colin MacLean and Kenneth Veitch (eds), *A Compendium of Scottish Ethnology*, Volume 2, *Religion*, Edinburgh: John Donald, an imprint of Birlinn.

Galt, John, 1821, *Annals of the Parish*, Rockville, MD: Serenity (2009).

Graham, H. G., 1937, *The Social Life of Scotland in the Eighteenth Century*, 4th edn., London: A. & C. Black.

Hazlett, Ian, Doug Gay and Douglas Galbraith, 2013, *A Usable Past? Belief, Worship and Song in Reformation Context*, Edinburgh: Church Service Society .

Hazlett, Ian, 2010, 'A New Version of the Scots Confession', *Theology in Scotland* 17:2.

Henderson, G.D., 1943, *Heritage: A Study of the Disruption*, Edinburgh: Oliver & Boyd.

Henderson, G. D., 1951, *The Claims of the Church of Scotland*, London: Hodder & Stoughton.

James, Kirk (ed.), 1980, *The Second Book of Discipline*, Edinburgh: Saint Andrew Press.

Jeal, Tim, 2013, *Livingstone*, rev. ed., New Haven, CT: Yale University Press.

Lamont, Stewart, 1991, *The Swordbreaker: John Knox and the European Reformation*, London: Hodder & Stoughton.

Leckie, J. H., 1925, *Fergus Ferguson: His Theology and Heresy Trial*, Edinburgh: T&T Clark.

Lyall, Francis, 1980, *Of Presbyters and Kings*, Aberdeen: Aberdeen University Press.

Macdonald, Finlay A. J., 1983, *Law and Doctrine in the Church of Scotland with Particular Reference to Confessions of Faith*, unpublished PhD thesis, Edinburgh: University of St Andrews.

Macdonald, Finlay A. J., 2004, *Confidence in a Changing Church*, Edinburgh: Saint Andrew Press.

Macdonald, Finlay A. J., 2012, *Luke Paul*, London: Shoving Leopard.

Macdonald, Finlay A. J., 2013, *Luke Paul and the Mosque*, Shoving Leopard.

McKay, Johnston R., 2012, *The Kirk and the Kingdom*, McKay, Johnston R., 2012, T*he Kirk and the Kingdom*, Edinburgh: Edinburgh University Press.

McKerrow, J., 1845, *History of the Secession Church*, Charleston, SC: Bibliolife (2009).

MacLean, Marjory M., 2009, *The Crown Rights of the Redeemer*, Edinburgh: Saint Andrew Press.

Marshall, Peter, 2015, 'Britain's Reformation', in Peter Marshall (ed.), *The Oxford Illustrated History of the Reformation*, Oxford: Oxford University Press.

Marshall, Rosalind K., 2001, *Mary of Guise*, Edinburgh: National Museum of Scotland Publishing.

Marshall, Rosalind K., 2008, *John Knox*, Edinburgh: Birlinn.

Marshall, Rosalind K., 2009, *St Giles' The Dramatic Story of a Great Church and its People*, Edinburgh: Saint Andrew Press.

Marshall, Rosalind K., 2010, *Mary Queen of Scots:Truth or Lies*, Edinburgh: Saint Andrew Press.

Marshall, Rosalind K., 2013, *Columba's Iona: A New History*, Dingwall: Sandstone Press.

Muirhead, Andrew T. M., 2015, *Reformation, Dissent and Diversity*, London: Bloomsbury.

Murray, Douglas, 1993, *Freedom to Reform*, Edinburgh: T&T Clark.

Patrick, Millar, 1949, *Four Centuries of Scottish Psalmody*, London: Oxford University Press.

Purser, John, 1992, *Scotland's Music*, Edinburgh: Mainstream. Publishing.

Reid, Harry, 2001, *Outside Verdict: A New Kirk in an Old Scotland*, Edinburgh: Saint Andrew Press.

Reid, Harry, 2016, *The Soul of Scotland*, Edinburgh: Saint Andrew Press.

Rodger, Lord Alan of Earlsferry, 2008, *The Courts, the Church and the Constitution*, Edinburgh: Edinburgh University Press.

Roper, Lyndol, 2015, 'Martin Luther', in Peter Marshall (ed.), *The Oxford Illustrated History of the Reformation*, Oxford: Oxford University Press.

Ross, Andrew C., 2006, 'Missions and Missionaries: Foreign', in Colin MacLean and Kenneth Veitch (eds), *A Compendium of Scottish Ethnology*, Volume 12, *Religion*, Edinburgh: John Donald, an imprint of Birlinn.

Ross, J. M., 1960, *Four Centuries of Scottish Worship*, London: Presbyterian Historical Society of England.

Sefton, Henry R., 2006, 'Occasions in the Reformed Church', in Colin MacLean and Kenneth Veitch (eds), *A Compendium of Scottish Ethnology*, Volume 12, *Religion*. John Donald, an imprint of Birlinn.

Scott, D., 1886, *Annals and Statistics of the Original Secession Church*, A Elliot.

Sjölinder, R., 1962, *Presbyterian Reunion in Scotland*, Edinburgh: T&T Clark.

Struthers, Gavin, 1843, *The History of the Rise, Progress, and Principles of The Relief Church*, Glasgow: Fullarton & Co.

Weatherhead, James L., 1997, *The Constitution and Laws of the Church of Scotland*, Edinburgh: Board of Practice and Procedure.

Whyte, Ian, 2006, 'Ministers and Society in Scotland' 1560-1800', in Colin MacLean and Kenneth Veitch (eds), *A Compendium of Scottish Ethnology*, Volume 12, *Religion*, Edinburgh: John Donald, an imprint of Birlinn.

Woodside, David, 1910, *The Soul of a Scottish Church, or the Contribution of the United Presbyterian Church to Scottish Life and Religion*, Edinburgh: United Free Church Publishing.

Wotherspoon, H. J. and Kirkpatrick, J. M., 1960, *A Manual of Church Doctrine according to the Church of Scotland*, rev. edn by T. F. Torrance and R. S. Wright, Oxford University Press.

INDEX OF NAMES AND SUBJECTS

The Holy Fair (Burns) 111
Holyrood 3, 13, 40, 41, 54, 56, 182, 209
Home, John 121; *Douglas* 120
homosexuality
    'A Challenge to Unity' 188; clergy and 212–13; debates 187–8; decriminalisation of 186–7; Rennie's case 188–9
Honest to God (Robinson) 191
Hood, Dr Lorna 176
Horne, Janet 86
Hume, David 120, 121
Hutcheson, Francis 100
Hutcheson, Revd James 86
Hutton, James 121

India, 20th c. ecumenicalism 177; missions in 129
indulgences, controversy over 5; Luther and 7–8; Luther's outrage over 67, 68
Inglis, Dr, of Greyfriars 143–84
Innes, Taylor 160; negotiating union 167
Innocent VIII, Pope, James IV and 3
Institutes of Religion (Calvin) 115
The Institutes of the Christian Religion (Calvin) 21
International Missionary Council 177
Iona, historical and legal status 183–6
Iona Wild Goose Group 196
Ireland, Easter Rising 204; Irish emigrants in Scotland 204
Irvine, Revd Euphemia 174
Irving, Edward 148; heresy of 132–3

Jacobites 81–2; Bonnie Prince Charlie 104; Glencoe massacre 91
James III 2
James IV
    life and death of 2–6; marries Margaret Tudor 5
James the Pretender, biding time 90
James V and II 6
    Catholic loyalty 10–13; church reforms 11; Monmouth and 79; succeeds Charles II 79, 80

James VI and I
    Authorised Bible 51; birth of 41; brings the Reformation 167; coronation 41; death of 54; Elizabeth leaves throne to 52; Lennox and 47–8; Melville on Christ's sovereignty 47; Ruthven raid 48–9
James VII and II
    death of 90; loses the throne 80–1
Jesus Christ
    doctrine of transubstantiation 23
John Paul II, Pope 180
John XXIII, Pope 179
Johnson, Dr Samuel 184
Johnson, Robert (composer) 35–6
Johnston, Archibald 59, 90
Johnston, Robert (composer) 35, 129
Judaism, ecumenicalism and 181–2
Julius II, Pope 4

Keith, William, 25
Kesting, Dr Sheilagh 176
King of Martyrs, John Glas 116–17
kings, divine right of 55
Knox, John
    Book of Common Order 57; Calvin and 24; death of 44; in England 18, 19–20; *First Blast of the Trumpet* 27–8, 29; in Frankfurt 24; in Geneva 25–8; *History of the Reformation* 5; leaves for Switzerland 20; marriage to Bowes 24–6; marries Margaret Stewart 44; Mary and 39–40; Mary of Guise and 28–30; monthly communion 111; Reformation texts 32–5; return to Scotland 28–30; role in Reformation 15–20; slavery and sanctuary 18
Knox, Marjorie (née Bowes) 18; death of 44; marries Knox 24, 26

Lamont, Dr David 143–4
Laud, Archbishop William
    insensitive to Scots 56–7; Prayer book of 58; Stafford and 64

Watt, James 121
Wedderburn brothers, *Godlie Psalms and Spirituall Sangis* 36
Welby, Archbishop, Dr Justin, Columba Declaration 181
Wellington, Sheena 209
Welsh, Dr David 139
Wesley, John, mission in Scotland 106–7
Westminster Confession 70; 20th c. reassessment 192–4; Auchterarder Creed and 97–8; churches' unity and 163–4; Declatory Act and 150; Ferguson's 'Creed Revision' heresy 148; Free Church and 163; interfaith relations and 182; origin of 66; union and 166; William of Orange and 83–5
White, John 165, 200; union of churches 170
Whitfield, George, Seceders and 105–6
Whyte, Professor James 206
William of Orange
Coronation Oath 83; death of 90; the Glorious Revolution 80–1; religious policies 81–4
Willock, John, Reformation texts 32
Wilson, John, Scottish Missionary Society 129
Wilson, Margaret, Scottish Missionary Society 129
Wilson, William, the Secession Church 102–3
Winning, Archbishop Tom 180
Winram, John 17–18, 30; office in Reformed Church 35; Reformation texts 32

Wishart, George 14; Knox and 15–16; sings at arrest 36
Witch Wood (Buchan) 86
witchcraft 23; 16th and 17th c. cases 85–6
Wode, Thomas, psalter of 37
Wolfenden, Sir John 186–7
Woman's Guild 172; foundation of 157–8; 'Mother God' prayer 198; restoration of Iona 184
women
20th c. changes 171–6; Diaconate scheme 158–9; Iona community and 185; 'Mother God' 198; Women's Guild 157–8
World Council of Churches
1952 Lund conference 179; San Antonio Declaration 182
World War I, union negotiations and 169
worship
18th c. differences 107–8; in 19th c. 143–8; 20th c. 194–9; 1560 form of 37–8; innovations 202–3; Knox and reforms 34; music and song 35–7; Presbyterian 144–6; statement of faith 215–16; union discussion and 165–6
Wotherspoon, A. W. 165, 166, 168
Wrestling with the Church (Levision) 176
Wright, Canon Kenyon 208
WWII, women and 172–3
Wycliffe, John 5

Young, Robert, Veto Act and 135–6

Zambia, Livingstones and 130, 131